Hector Guimard

"I came to think that art must be based on
science and that, in everything having to do
with artistic composition, the aim should
be the unity which is that of nature itself—
because the logic of nature is impeccable."

Hector Guimard

HECTOR GUIMARD

· PHOTOGRAPHS BY ·
FELIPE FERRÉ

· TEXT BY ·
MAURICE RHEIMS

· EXPLANATORY CAPTIONS AND CHRONOLOGY BY ·
GEORGES VIGNE

· HARRY N. ABRAMS, INC., PUBLISHERS, NEW YORK ·

Translated from the French by Robert Erich Wolf

Editor, English-language edition: Eric Himmel

Jacket and type design, English-language edition: Carol Robson

Library of Congress Cataloging-in-Publication Data

Ferré, Felipe, 1934–
  Hector Guimard.

  Translation of: Hector Guimard, archte. Rev. and enl.
  1. Guimard, Hector, 1867–1942—Criticism and interpre-
tation.   2. Art nouveau (Architecture)—France.
I. Guimard, Hector, 1867–1942.   II. Rheims, Maurice.
III. Title
NA1053.G8F4713   1987   720′.92′4   86–32232
ISBN 0-8109-0973-1

A Times Mirror Company

Printed and bound in Italy

Contents

FOREWORD

Why a book about Hector Guimard?

Because there are very few publications about him, and his work, even today, is known only to initiates, to persons whose business or pleasure it is to know about him. The very opposite of Antoni Gaudí, the inspired visionary of Barcelona and perhaps the most important Art Nouveau architect: for Spaniards, whatever their station in life, Gaudí is and always has been one of the greatest geniuses of art.

Guimard's work parallels that of Gaudí in a number of points. Each man on his own broke with the established norms of a classicism which, in their time, had sunk to a decadent academicism. Each did what he did with the aim of plunging full tilt into an all-out modernism.

Both Guimard and Gaudí were exceptional beings to whom no one can be indifferent. Steeped in Ruskin's naturalistic philosophy and the rationalistic theories of Viollet-le-Duc, each created a body of work on his own and all his own. Each was a brilliant draftsman. Out of an overflowing imagination each created new forms derived from nature. They shared an approach to architecture that was absolute, total: after working out a project on paper, each would realize it himself down to the smallest detail, from complex structural framework to the doorbell and even the street number on the front door.

So too for the interior decoration: stained-glass windows, hardware, furniture, carpets, tapestries, doorknobs, all of it. The prime example for Guimard is the Castel Béranger of 1894–98, for Gaudí the Casa Calvet of 1898–1900.

By mysterious and still-unexplained ways, the influence and tendencies of Art Nouveau spread in a relatively brief time throughout Europe and even to America with Louis Sullivan and the Chicago School. Each architect created an original body of work, without direct connection with what any other architect did, yet all part of a single current that formed a distinct style: Art Nouveau.

F. F.

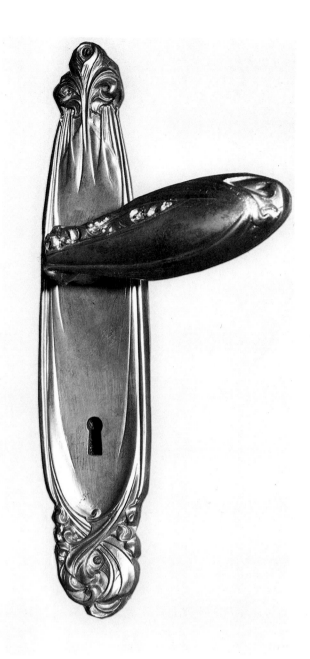

INTRODUCTION

Pavillon de l'Eléctricité
Exposition Universelle, Paris, 1889
(*Illustration from* La Construction Moderne, *March 22, 1889*)

Contrary to what the elaborate trappings of the pavilion might lead one to suppose, the building was by no means official and certainly not grandiose. At the most it served for a few demonstrations of electromagnetism. Yet one senses in it already the eclecticism of Guimard's first works, his liking for fantasy, for a picturesqueness which, here, takes the form of something between a church porch and a Swiss chalet. From the start his career would be marked by a long series of "castles."

In 1830 Quatremère de Quincy, pontiff of architecture, declared: We recognize as the true art of architecture only that which takes its roots and origins from Athens and then from Rome.

Never in the previous ten centuries had an architectural vacuum been so obvious, and this throughout the Western world. Seventy-five years earlier Claude-Nicolas Ledoux and Jacques-Ange Gabriel had been demonstrating that, in their discipline as in every other form of creation, the ring had never come full circle, that new ways would open with each step taken to explore them. But the contemporaries of Louis-Philippe only had a mind for political strategy and private finance. No matter if buildings were noble or not, so long as great arteries were laid out straight and broad, enabling the public powers, in the event of an uprising, to block the rioters from marching on the heart of the city. All of which was to the liking of the men of finance as well, who were forever demanding something new and then newer. Buildings rose higher and higher: with land becoming more and more expensive and building costs soaring, whatever was built was meant to last. To a well-off clientele real estate owners offered vast spaces in graceless buildings, while the petty bourgeoisie had to make do with the sempiternal living room, dining room, two bedrooms, kitchen-and-pantry.

The quest for Beauty cost time and money. On façades indistinguishable from those of barracks, an occasional lion's head might be plastered or niches carved to house caryatids shivering in the cold.

It was the same everywhere: Paris, London, Vienna. The well-heeled client demanded something "serious," respected only handcut stone, turned up his nose at brick. What he admired was no longer the Beautiful but the *comme il faut*, the "right" thing. In London the façades had to be Victorian, in Paris à la Haussmann, in Munich the dream was of the century of Pericles, in Vienna they didn't beat about the bush and the style approved by Franz Joseph and his functionaries was baptized "bureaucratic," plain and simple. People blessed with real fortunes were scarcely better served, and the sublime objects bankers who had made it big only yesterday could now afford were displayed in hodgepodge mansions in Alhambra-Rambouillet-Chenonceaux style. The Englishman Joseph Paxton carried the day with outright eclecticism, putting up dwellings just right for Jules Verne's heroes or for madmen made of money.

In Paris the Opéra conjured up the kind of sublime dream a Roman emperor and one of Verdi's heroines might share in the same night. Charles Garnier, baroque from head to toenails, was a genius in many respects, a sort of Tiepolo of architecture, but he remained very much a man of the Establishment. Fascinated by the society that frequented the Tuileries or Compiègne, by luxury and lavishness, he could not help but veto the projects of younger colleagues who preferred raw iron girders to marble, bronze, and stucco: "shed-builders," the gentlemen of the Academy dubbed them. The clientele, the man in the street, attached with all his heart and mind to the familiar notions of yesteryear, was all too willing to share those sentiments: Our past is so rich, why look for anything else?

Paris, despite the teachings of Victor Baltard, Léon Vaudoyer, and Viollet-le-Duc, continued to line its streets with façades designed by architects still obsessed with the Great Men of the Past. Vitruvius, Bramante, Le Vau, Gabriel never built rental property, but that didn't matter: one could always imagine them at the drawing tables of the 1880s, busily at work designing Parc Monceau, Auteuil, or Passy.

The results—in the hundreds—are there before our eyes. Although the whole lot of it is lacking in grace and imagination, in a hundred years boulevards Haussmann, Péreire, or Malesherbes will nevertheless have taken on the nobility of time, will touch our hearts like old folks driveling away at their memories.

As early as 1860 a few voices rose in challenge, Viollet-le-Duc's among them. The man was listened to so much the more because he did not turn a stony gaze on everything done before. He considered those pages admirably illustrated but that it was time to turn them. Young architects fed up with the teaching at the Beaux-Arts listened with amazement to this man so much a part of his century who nonetheless was inviting them to think things through, to meditate on them. Viollet-le-Duc was the first to extol asymmetry, the first to study ground plans and elevations in terms of form, the first to recommend using new materials: let us stop dismissing cast iron and steel as "vulgar" elements, he urged, because it is precisely those great flexible metals that can be bent to the exigencies of modernity and Beauty.

His *Entretiens sur l'Art* ("Conversations about Art") appeared prophetic to the rising generation. They were viewed as prayers for a new Acropolis: You, the young, seize the chances your epoch offers you.

Certainly Viollet-le-Duc and Garnier were the two greatest architects of the latter half of the century. With a difference in age of a scant ten years or so, they were practically contemporaries. Yet, on the plane of aesthetics, centuries separate them. Garnier belonged to a world long past, Viollet-le-Duc had eyes only for the future.

When the young Hector Guimard emerged from the Ecole des Beaux-Arts in 1889, he was twenty-two. He appears to have left before taking his diploma. To him, as to many of his fellow-students, eclecticism no longer seemed anything but a pale imitation of antiquity. He had learned from Viollet-le-Duc that art can progress only in the "living milieu of the Nation." For him, the builder of Pierrefonds was the only master whose teaching appeared to be in line with the times.

Once again it was the first revolutionaries who faced the first fire. Around 1890 the apostles of iron as a building material would be sufficiently sure of themselves to refuse thenceforth to conceal their construction behind outdated masks borrowed from Byzantium or the medieval West. Once the young architects had got rid of those "false friends" they could finally respond to the aspirations of the new century in birth.

Luck was with Guimard. One can imagine how the young man freshly arrived from his provincial Lyonnais home felt about a Paris where the superannuated graybeards of the Salon—Cabanel, Bouguereau, Bonnat, and their ilk—were beginning to lose ground. And people were recognizing that the real talent belonged to the Impressionists. To be an artist in Paris in 1890 meant having the privilege of encountering Signac, Seurat, Degas, Rodin, and so many others.

Once he had completed his studies, providence offered the young Guimard two tickets: one to Great Britain, the other to Brussels.

London was emerging brutally from its past. The city was changing before one's eyes. But there too one had to be prudent. The Londoners' taste was still inclined to

Detail of a door, Hôtel Mezzara

Marquee
5 bis avenue Foch, Saint-Cloud
1907–08 (destroyed)

This delicate marquee was designed for a building in Saint-Cloud, where it sheltered the door to the garden. The original door, also by Guimard, is now in the collection of the Musée d'Orsay, Paris. Even in such a modest task Guimard could display his talent to the full, here by no more than the adroit twisting of a few standardized iron bars.

the Victorian. Young architects like Charles Townsend, Charles Voysey, and James MacLaren still had to be wary of the judgment of the man in the street. Only the informed passersby would notice their aspiration toward something ever more modern.

In Brussels, no such scruples. The Belgians, whom we French have a foolish tendency to make fun of, at the end of last century were well and truly ahead of us in matters intellectual as well as artistic. Modern Brussels was less than a half-century old. It was the youngest of the capitals, and so its architects had the luck of finding much of it not yet built over. Victor Horta and Paul Hankar showed their young French colleague what they were up to: the Hôtel Tassel was still under construction and the future Hôtel Solvay still on the drawing table. Brilliant scions of Art Nouveau! For more than ten years their star would shine supreme, and it has never ceased to enchant us.

Back in Paris, Guimard felt his wings growing stronger. Now he could get a bird's-eye view of the old world that was passing and salvage from it, at a pinch, an occasional handsome motif. His first building jobs were entrusted to him, and soon it sufficed for him merely to think "façade" for his inspiration to supply him with ideas for house fronts that unfurled, that turned and twisted with elfin grace under his loving gaze. On his working diagrams, on his blueprints, the stones took to dancing: do with us as you wish, they seemed to say, we are clay in a sculptor's hand.

Guimard's edifices, their exterior and interior structures, reveal how very complex his approach was. In chatty articles published regularly in the review *Architecture* Louis-Charles Boileau, a contemporary of Art Nouveau, tried to define the importance that decoration had with regard to the building itself in Guimard's thinking. Although the ornamentation involves relatively numerous sculptured elements, Boileau wrote, one need not look for anything precise, for any motif written in a clear and eloquent handwriting. Leaving aside the relationship between the decoration and the building's fundamental structure, he spoke of "decoration in the form of flames, waves, fluid and subtle," and he added that Guimard's major concern was with "catching at just the right places, by more or less copious setbacks, a solid stuff that tends to flow away too rapidly to create finally ensembles of perfect picturesqueness." In this, however, Boileau may be playing the young creator of the Castel Béranger false. Critics and historians likewise mix things up, fail to grasp that the nature of Guimard had scarcely anything in common with what, at the same time, was coming to fascinate the craftsmen artists of the School of Nancy and those who, in Italy, were taking part in the Floreal movement. Henri Frantz, in the *Magazine of Art* in 1901, got things right when he wrote that Guimard's ambition was "to escape completely from all ornament directly borrowed from nature, or to put it shortly, from floral design . . . . Line alone is what M. Guimard relies on; he gets all his effects from the use of 'line' or combinations of lines."

As often in such cases, we have no idea how the Parisians first came to take Guimard to their hearts. Perhaps necessity played a part, but fashion no less. Whatever the case, our architect seems to have appeared on the scene in time to respond to new aesthetic propensities. Be that as it may, the Paris art world of that time was more cautious than today: not until Guimard won first prize in the contest for façade designs organized by the city of Paris did the public turn their attention to him and his Castel Béranger.

A few broad-minded spirits, a few patrons with taste, instead of fixing their choice once again on building plans that were half medieval, a quarter Regency, and the rest Louis XIII, took the risk of entrusting Guimard (as others would do with Jules Lavirotte) with the task of designing and erecting their buildings.

The press on the whole was favorable. It hailed the architect capable of freeing the French from the "English style reigning till now." Octave Uzanne, a much respected authority, wrote in 1898 in the *Echo de Paris*: "In Brussels we already had the astonishing Horta. May Monsieur Hector Guimard soon become our French Horta."

Guimard would begin with the outlying Auteuil quarter of Paris as his field of maneuver. His successes would be due, in the first place, to economic and social factors. In 1890 the price of building lots on the Plaine Monceau was soaring, and the Passy quarter was in full expansion. But Auteuil still belonged to the rural area of the capital, and around the place de l'Eglise there were still a few farms and vacant lots were plentiful. Places like that, so recently still "country" or provincial, cried to be exploited. For young architects they were a godsend, the more so since new neighborhoods called for a new architecture. By 1896 Auteuil was enamored of Art Nouveau; by 1910 there were already two or three hundred buildings in that style. Among the many builders who worked between place du Trocadéro and the porte de Saint-Cloud, Guimard holds first place with thirty-two edifices. To get the picture we can stroll through the part of the 16th arrondissement that centers on the rue La Fontaine and the rue George-Sand. Beginning on rue Molitor we reach the avenue de Versailles, then turn right on boulevard Exelmans and come back by rue Chardon-Lagache, making our way to the avenue Mozart. After a short detour for a glimpse of rue Henri-Heine, we follow avenue Mozart toward rue Greuze, ending up not far from the Trocadéro.

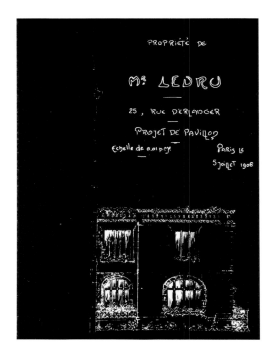

Project for a pavilion
25 rue d'Erlanger, Paris 16e
1908 (not built)

An aggressive architecture! Some writers hailed it with admiration, others felt a certain malaise. The critics, true to form, were divided. André Hallays wrote in 1899 in *La Construction Moderne*: "One sees well, one sees too much, those thoughts that absorbed the architect: his *idée fixe* which reveals itself everywhere, from the vestibule door to the rooftop, is to break with all traditions and to protest against all conventions. Noble intentions; but continual protest, unreflecting protest, soon becomes intolerable, just like the worst of routines! It is well and truly a nightmare of a house." For *Art et Décoration*, quite the contrary: "The construction produces somewhat the effect of a work of a lost civilization suddenly re-emerging into the light."

By the end of World War I the page had turned. The "Style 1925"—Art Déco— had been awaiting its hour since 1913 and now went on the offensive. The time had come when Guimard would be banished to the desert. Commissions became rare, he turned out a few buildings still marked by his personality but just as much concerned with catching up with what was now considered modern. One might say he overdid it, was prepared to pay any price to withstand the threats of fashion and the time. No use: the audacious sexagenarian was put on the shelf; the time of the real estate vultures had arrived. One André Rousseaux, a hack writer, announced in June, 1949, in *Art et Médécine*: "In architecture as in literature we are climbing back again from a low point indeed. We are emerging from the sloughs of 1900. There was perhaps no more miserable epoch in all the history of French architecture than that of Modern Style, of vermicelli in delirium, of the first Métro stations, of the Grand-Palais, of buildings covered in pastry-icing and tarted up with ceramic mascarons." True, others went under the guillotine at the same time: Emile Gallé, Louis Majorelle, Charles Rennie MacKintosh, Josef Hoffmann, and so many others. But happily they were not written off altogether. The critic Louis Cheronnet wrote in 1932: "Let us not rush to be done with them. Rehabilitations do take place . . . and Apollo, god of arts, will always end up returning to those who belong to him. . . . In spite of all our judgments our grandchildren around 1970 and 1980 will go tracking down the bibelots of 1900, will smile at their superannuated forms and begin to collect them. . . . That is why I ask protection for the houses on rue La Fontaine, on avenue Rapp, for the interiors of the Restaurant Lucas Carton and the Bar Maxim's. To envisage the conservation of those vestiges seems to me just and useful; I would even, and I say this without laughing, like to see a Métro entrance put under protection, if only in the name of the history of Paris."

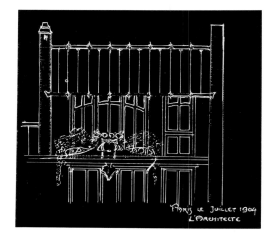

Project for raising the height of a hôtel
22 rue Chardon-Lagache, Paris 16e
1904

By 1960 the Surrealists were up in arms. Dali gave his blessing to "the prophetic ornamentation of Guimard as against the total lack of eroticism of the Le Corbusiers and other mental defectives of our decidedly woeful modern architecture."

The Guimard adventure lasted scarcely more than fifteen years, a little longer than that of Art Nouveau itself. If a few of his buildings survive, we can thank providence for it more than man: the crises in finance and real estate meant that there was less pressure to bulldoze those relics of the past and replace them with profitable income properties.

That situation, however, was not fated to last. A few years ago there were rumors that the Castel Henriette was to be torn down, one of the most ravishing of Guimard's creations, comparable in its eccentricity to the finest "follies" of times past. André Malraux was minister of culture at the time. I went to see him. I begged him to stop that massacre.

"Castel Henriette! Don't know it," said Malraux. "Guimard. . . . You like that stuff?" came next. "No reason to prevent its destruction." I protested, but he cut me short: "Everyone to his own nasty taste!" A few weeks later the contractors had destroyed this precious monument of the past, and now only a few elements survive here and there in museums abroad.

Nothing predisposed me to write about an architectural movement of modern times. That is not my "line of work." But the beauty of Felipe Ferré's photographs, the originality of his angles and framings, his feelings for the building materials which the lens captures infinitely better than the eye, incited me to reflect somewhat more about certain moments of our history when the French, so addicted to logic even in the domain of Beauty, took genuine pleasure in relaxing that constraint and living under the reign of a new baroque and a short-lived mannerism.

Leaf through this book, discover these houses, think about man's inventive genius. Buildings . . . ? More than that: astonishing objects, full of grace, often pertly witty, worthy of a place in my—and your—curiosity cabinet.

HOTEL ROSZE

34 RUE BOILEAU
PARIS 16E

1891

Guimard was twenty-four when he built this private dwelling. There was no talk yet of Art Nouveau, but already in Nancy, in Great Britain, in Belgium, people had dreamed of a new art. In architecture Viollet-le-Duc had proposed that the Gothic had not said its last word, that it had not died, could still provide a new source of inspiration. In 1891 Guimard's sole ambition was to follow in the footsteps of the architect who had died twelve years earlier. While the masters of the old school would likely enough find a good deal here not to their taste, the builder of Pierrefonds would have found nothing to criticize in his young admirer's work.

In rue Boileau it was best for Guimard to move cautiously. The venerable street had two centuries of history behind it. Boileau had lived at number 26, Hubert Robert at number 20. Which meant that however eager the young architect might be to exercise his taste for modernity, he had to go about it discreetly, reserving his real inventions for the interior. The façade is elegant, simple: in Italy it would be called pseudo-Florentine. The only brilliant note comes from the subtle play of different tonalities, in which ocher dominates but is interrupted here and there by the insertion of elements in siliceous sandstone and by a few turquoise glazed bricks. The "bell tower" is massive but discreet, the peaked roof over the front gate is laid with tiles whose colors match nicely those of the roofs. Already there is no hint of symmetry; the windows are of different shapes and sizes, and are marked off by borders of brick, stone, or terracotta.

Here we are far from Garnier's sumptuosity but also from what Guimard would imagine five or six years on for his Castel Béranger and, two decades later, for the enchanting and elegant Hôtel Mezzara.

As the earliest of Guimard's works that survive, the Hôtel Roszé is the inevitable point of departure for any study of his work. It offers touching evidence of what he could do with what he learned at the Ecole des Beaux-Arts. Indeed, until just before he built the Castel Béranger in 1894–98 he continued to take part in that venerable institution's prize competitions. Here the façade has numerous references to styles of the past but in such chaos that only the materials used ensure a consistent visual impression. Among those materials, brick and siliceous sandstone would remain among the constants of his architectural language to the end of his career.

Detail of the main façade

General view

HOTEL JASSEDE

41 RUE CHARDON-LAGACHE
PARIS 16E

1893

Picturesque. . . . The image of naiveté. . . . So one thinks passing by this little house on rue Chardon-Lagache. From year to year since 1890 the 16th arrondissement had been changing from its country green to the beige and rose of building materials: construction was going in full force. We are in 1893 and the Hôtel Jassedé, conceived two years ago, will be finished in a few months. If its style echoes the historicist taste of the moment, and if charm is its chief feature, the house nonetheless strikes one as original yet imprinted with modesty, as if timidity ensured protection for its superiority. What is audacious is the massive use of brick, a material which the French north of the Loire have never considered distinguished. The same for siliceous sandstone, reserved as a rule for the basement stories of buildings of no pretensions, though widely used on those charming little houses which still girdle the Parisian suburbs by the hundreds.

The Hôtel Jassedé is built directly on the street. A droll touch: the pediment over the entrance gate, no doubt meant as a last wink at the neo-medievalism of the time. The top-story windows, in what used to be called the *chambres de bonne*, the maids' rooms, are surmounted by odd little roofs rather like the bonnets worn by the Demoiselles Fenouillard, the heroines of familiar French children's books.

As he would never cease to do from then on, here Guimard took pleasure in contrasting glazed bricks with bricks straight from the kiln. Here and there, ceramic panels decorated with floral motifs, turned out in the workshops of Emile Müller & Co., remind us how much the Symbolist style was still in vogue.

The ironwork looks simple, but an experienced eye can already pick out certain singularities.

Though the project is more ambitious here, the young Guimard is still no more capable of curbing his enthusiasms than in the Hôtel Roszé. The plan is still complicated (though it has logic behind it), the coloring is enriched by ceramic elements, and the ironwork is particularly elaborate and already entirely personal and novel in design; close to an Art Nouveau which some still maintain, mistakenly, was a style absent from Guimard's work until after he met the Belgian architect Victor Horta in 1895.

At first limited to suburban homes, Guimard's architecture was still much like what other people of the time were building in such comfortably-off small towns around Paris as Saint-Cloud, Le Vésinet, or Garches, which would be his center of activity as well for a while. If his first creations in Paris strike us as surprising today, in an Auteuil now totally urbanized, when they were built they fitted perfectly into the sort of picturesque landscape or townscape typical of middle-class suburban residential zones. It was only in occasional details and in his close concern with every part and element of the edifice that our architect revealed himself as an innovator.

Front gate

Garden façade

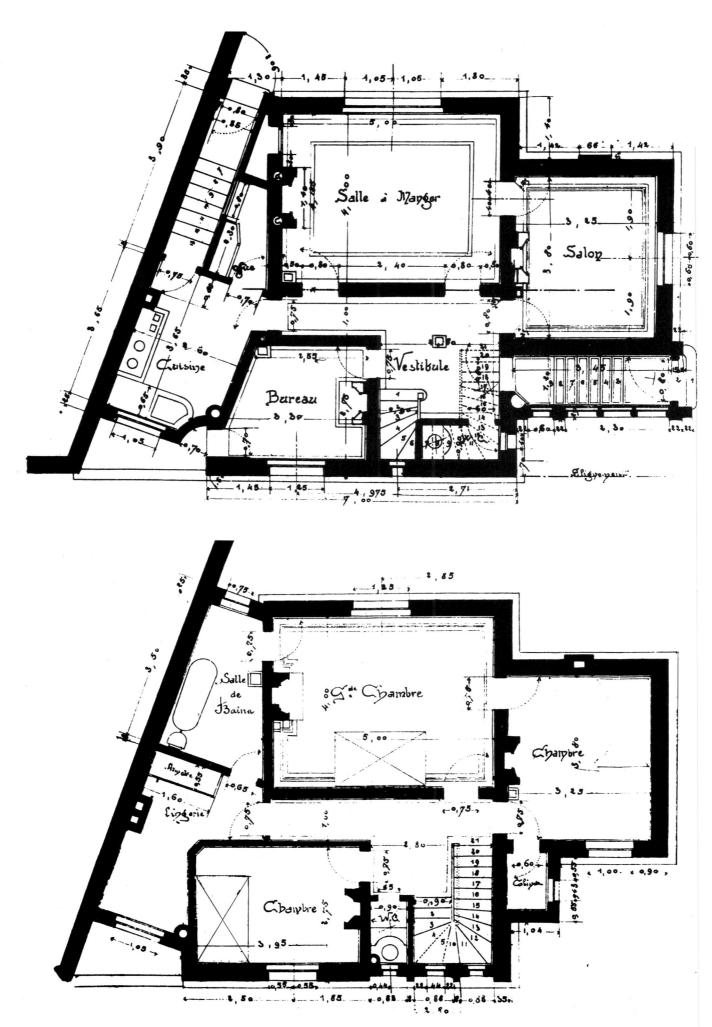

Ground plans of the first and second floors

Side view

Overleaf: Two watercolors by Guimard published by Victor Champier in *L'Art Décoratif Moderne* (1899)

Especially when their memories of their years at the Ecole des Beaux-Arts were still fresh, architects sometimes amused themselves by drawing their works in full perspective view and with a good dose of fantasy. It is no doubt relevant that Guimard was himself a professor when these drawings were done. One easily recognizes the Hôtel Jassedé, but in a curious surrounding of greenery: the architect gave free rein to his daydreams to the point of forgetting that the house faced a perfectly ordinary street.

22 HÔTEL JASSEDÉ

PRIVATE HOUSE

63 AVENUE DU GÉNÉRAL DE GAULLE
ISSY-LES-MOULINEAUX (HAUTS-DE-SEINE)

1893

This house in the Parisian left-bank suburb of Issy-les-Moulineaux was conceived around 1893 and is particularly interesting for both its discretion and its originality. By siting the building at a slight angle to the street Guimard conveyed the impression that it was meant as something out of the ordinary. The house does project, but by a few degrees only and with delicacy, timidly, as if fearful of offending its neighbors.

Viewed from the entrance gate the construction presents itself in three planes: a first focused on the main door; a second with two windows, one on the ground floor, the other on the second floor; a third culminating in three round-arched windows. Tall chimneys placed audaciously rise here and there from the roofs.

The building is in siliceous sandstone, a material that would never lose its appeal for Guimard. Like family jewels worn with discretion by an elegant woman, a few warm-toned elements in ceramic stand out as something precious against the plain sandstone. An ornamental motif taking the form of an orange-colored half-apple framed in light green and set into squares of steely blue ceramic was designed by Guimard and produced in Müller's kilns; it was still featured his company's catalogue in 1904. Wrought- or cast-iron grilles with elegant arabesques, also painted in warm tones, separate the house from the street.

General view

More modest than the two preceding houses, this small dwelling was nonetheless conceived on the basis of the same ideas: note the combination of very different materials, the avoidance of a single plane for the façade, the complicated treatment of the roofs. The suburban environment in which the house is situated remains practically unchanged since the start of the century, making it possible to see how attentive Guimard was to integrating his work into an existing site with its own characteristics.

Details of the roofs

The front door

HOTEL DELFAU

1894

The Hôtel Delfau is charming, old-fashioned, banal, still rock-solid. If it had not been built by Guimard would it deserve our attention?

Everything suggests that the still-green environment of Auteuil in 1894 incited Guimard to think in country terms. Rue Molitor was practically in the suburbs, and the situation of the Hôtel Delfau at the time must have been rather like that of the houses in the eastern part of the capital which today still swarm along the banks of the Marne.

Medieval traits linger on in the façade with its comfortably bourgeois bow to the Gothic. Not narrow openings but broad windows flood the main rooms with light. What is original here is the triangular gable on the top story, with the recessed windows so frequent since the Middle Ages. This is something Guimard learned on his visit to London in 1894. Later, the architect Charles Holden, who built the Belgrave Hospital in 1903, took up the idea. It is found also on the Villa Majorelle in Nancy, designed by Henri Sauvage, and the Villa Floria in Palermo, designed by Ernesto Basile, who wished to temper the fierce Sicilian sunlight and give a little shade to the rooms within.

The façade on rue Molitor is in freestone and two-toned ocher brick. Rather than brighten the ensemble with floral decorations or fantastic animals, Guimard chose a cock for which Guérin designed the motif and Muller glazed and baked the ceramic. The cock, of course, was meant to strike a very French, patriotic, diehard note; this same cock which Edmund Rostand would make the subject of his verse-play *Chantecler* (1910).

As we know from a postcard brought out around 1920, the private dwelling was soon transformed into a nursing home, the "Hygiene Home" (in English), whose proprietor Dr. Albiousse made it plain in a publicity leaflet that he took neither mental nor contagious patients. That document also shows that over the years the house had suffered profound modification, including the addition of a left wing built around 1920 by the architect François Orliac.

From the somewhat encyclopedic picturesqueness to which Guimard's work had been prone until now—Moorish arches in the Hôtel Roszé, an almost Anglo-Saxon austerity in the house in Issy-les-Moulineaux—the Hôtel Delfau stands out as something different. It is a little-known work, sometimes looked down on, yet it shows for the first time how totally homogeneous Guimard could make his constructions, a factor of key importance throughout his career. On the other hand, here is his first timid try at the "castles" to come, notably in the very medieval verticals of the main bay of the façade. But as we see it today its simplicity is exaggerated, because when François Orliac added a neo-Gothic wing on the left he removed the grille and main doorway.

Prospectus for
the Hygiene Home

Régimes, Convalescences, A
Repos, Neurasthénie. De 20 à
chauffage, éclairage, blanchissage
ordinaire de l'Etablissement.
NI ALIÉNÉS, NI CONTAG
Ouvert à tout le Corps Médi
le Docteur de la Clinique.

Cock decorating the pediment over the second-story window

The request for authorization to build made in September, 1894, is evidence that the Hôtel Delfau was conceived immediately before the Castel Béranger. The difference of program for the two projects—and above all the time required to build each of them—meant that in outward appearance the buildings would be totally dissimilar. Nonetheless, we can consider the little house on rue Molitor as a small Castel Béranger in a first version; as what the architect might have produced for the latter had he abided by his now unknown initial project.

HYGIENE HOME

MAISON de RÉGIMES du **Docteur d'ALBIOUSSE**, 1 bis et 1 ter, Rue Molitor, PARIS, (XVIᵉ) - Téléph. : **629.14.**

Moyens de Communications :

Chemin de fer de ceinture : Saint-Lazare à Auteuil ; Tramways : Auteuil-Madeleine, Auteuil-Saint Sulpice, Boulogne-Auteuil, Champ de Mars-Auteuil, Louvre-Versailles.

CLINIQUE ULTRA-MODERNE

Chauffage central, électricité, salles de bains, eau froide et eau chaude dans chaque chambre ainsi que le téléphone ; Nettoyage par le Vide, Jardin.

, Diathèses, Intoxications, Maladies de la Nutrition,

cs par jour, comprenant : Chambre meublée, nourriture, de lit, de toilette et de table ; service et soins du personnel

s Malades conservent leurs médecins et sont surveillés par

Street façade

CASTEL BERANGER

14 RUE LA FONTAINE
PARIS 16E

1894-98

One of the group of buildings raised by Guimard between 1894 and 1910 in a limited area of the 16th arrondissement, the Castel Béranger is without doubt a major masterwork of French Art Nouveau.

Until 1860, Auteuil was still a country place, inhabited by a rural population and a few eccentrics who found it pleasant. Soon, however, the quarter would become a choice place to live for an important fraction of the better Parisian bourgeoisie. If on May 10, 1871, a window had been open at 96 rue La Fontaine, a passerby could have heard the wailing of a newborn infant: Marcel Proust. At number 10 in the same street, as the Castel Béranger was being completed a few steps away, Guillaume Apollinaire was just moving in; it is there he met Marie Laurencin. At number 11 still lurked the shades of the sculptor James Pradier and his mistress Juliette Drouet, who soon formed a liaison with Victor Hugo that was to last until her death.

She must have been a bold one, a lover of things extraordinary, this Madame Fournier, the widow who owned the lot, to accept the plans that the still-young and practically unknown architect proposed to her. She got her reward in 1899 when her building won the competition organized by the city of Paris for the best façade conceived that year.

At first the press did not emphasize the modernity of the building but rather its medievalizing note: Once again a Gothic revival, they wrote, and at the time that implied no disapproval. The reaction must have been the same in Barcelona when Gaudí built his church of La Sagrada Familia.

Looking at the buildings framing the Castel Béranger, one can better understand Guimard's ambition to move beyond his century. Number 8-ter in the same street, with its Symbolist fronton and eternal lion chewing a ring, is a typical Second Empire façade. However, its use of two-toned bricks rising above a granite base must have persuaded Guimard not to make a total break with the neighboring houses and to utilize the same materials. Thus he built the first two stories and the part at the left in stone and, for the rest, chose pale pinkish bricks. That diversity is found also on the side overlooking the Hameau and on the back, reserved for the "service," bringing a lively note to those parts of a building most architects neglect.

A man of our time, Guimard did not permit his aesthetic conceptions to blind him to financial imperatives. With the cost of the land in mind, he saw to it that not an inch was wasted: for the concierge's loge he inserted a wall-sofa that fitted into the decor in a bend of the staircase. To attract tenants it was not enough to make things "nice" or "unusual"; the apartments had to be bright, and so the upper stories are set back to admit more light to those below them.

One doesn't "enter" the Castel Béranger. One slips into it, as is so also in most of the buildings Guimard would design subsequently. Here, as later, sharp angles are avoided, and lines simulate forms found in nature regardless of the material utilized,

(continued on page 36)

A complex work, the first income property Guimard built, the Castel Béranger remains beyond a doubt its author's most celebrated work. Commissioned by Monsieur Fournier as a small building (whose appearance will probably never be known to us), after that gentleman's death it became in the hands of his widow a major real estate and financial operation. In the three years that it was under construction Guimard, an astute politician, was able to put through, little by little and each in turn, every change he recommended to his client, above all in the details, down to the most seemingly insignificant.

On close inspection the building—or buildings, as there are actually two connected buildings with a courtyard between them—proves not yet truly unified. Here and there the decoration was rather artificially applied to a structure which was, all told, much like those Guimard had built before, and the Castel Béranger closed this epoch in his career brilliantly. Yet in the final reckoning it was precisely through such decoration that Guimard would make his name as an avant-garde architect. A fertile inventor in the domains of interior decoration, furniture and furnishings, stained glass, and ironwork, he would describe himself as the one-man band for a new era and a new clientele without cultural roots; a clientele for whom the adoption of a "new art," an Art Nouveau, could ensure social recognition. It should not be forgotten, however, that the Castel Béranger, for us a priceless manifesto of new developments in art (an idea very well orchestrated and put about by its author himself), was in its time only a medium-rent apartment building, without all the conveniences taken for granted in present-day low-cost public housing.

Entrance

Detail of a bow window

Plaque commemorating the award won by the façade

Detail of stonecarving over the entrance

One of the pillars of the enclosure giving on the Hameau Béranger

Street number of the building

Wrought-iron grille at the entrance

Left: General view of the main façade

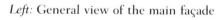

This page, clockwise from top left: Details of the street façade: Third-story balcony whose cast-iron balustrade is an example of the "Japanism" fashionable at the time. (Might the faces represent the architect himself?); Small window on the ground floor; Small window on the ground floor; Air vent; Cast-iron sea horse; Air vent

whether wood or metal. As Guimard himself repeated often, his aim was to bring out "the relationship with the branch": the branches of trees are not square, no angles exist in the forest. Scorning parallelism and symmetry—nothing of the sort is found in the world of plants—he observed that "forms generate themselves with movements that are never the same."

On a number of occasions Guimard attempted to explain his architectural conceptions, the problems he had had to overcome, his concern with an aesthetic based on the resistance of materials. But the press and broad public born to the rule of symmetry could scarcely get into their heads that a house could be treated as a sculptor treats clay. Guimard had a very modern feel for publicity. He would profit from winning the competition in 1899 by organizing in the same year an exhibition entirely devoted to his Castel Béranger. The architect, well connected with *Figaro*, received journalists and even brought out postcards of which the most popular showed him at work in his own studio, whose decoration he had himself dubbed "Style Guimard." He even organized guided tours of the building.

Right from the entrance the effect is one of surprise. Framed in carved sandstone, balanced by two columns, the doorway puts one in mind of a Cordovan alcazar rebuilt by a Romanesque architect. Pass through the superb door giving onto rue La Fontaine and you enter a vestibule lined on either side with glazed ceramic panels whose greenish tonalities appear at times coppered. Bricks straight from the kiln or glazed, all ceramic elements were for Guimard what gems are for the jeweler. Then too, in order

(*continued on page 41*)

Below: Shed roof over the side entrance

Right: Bow window

Opposite page: Elevation of the main façade on the rue La Fontaine before the decoration and doorway were modified

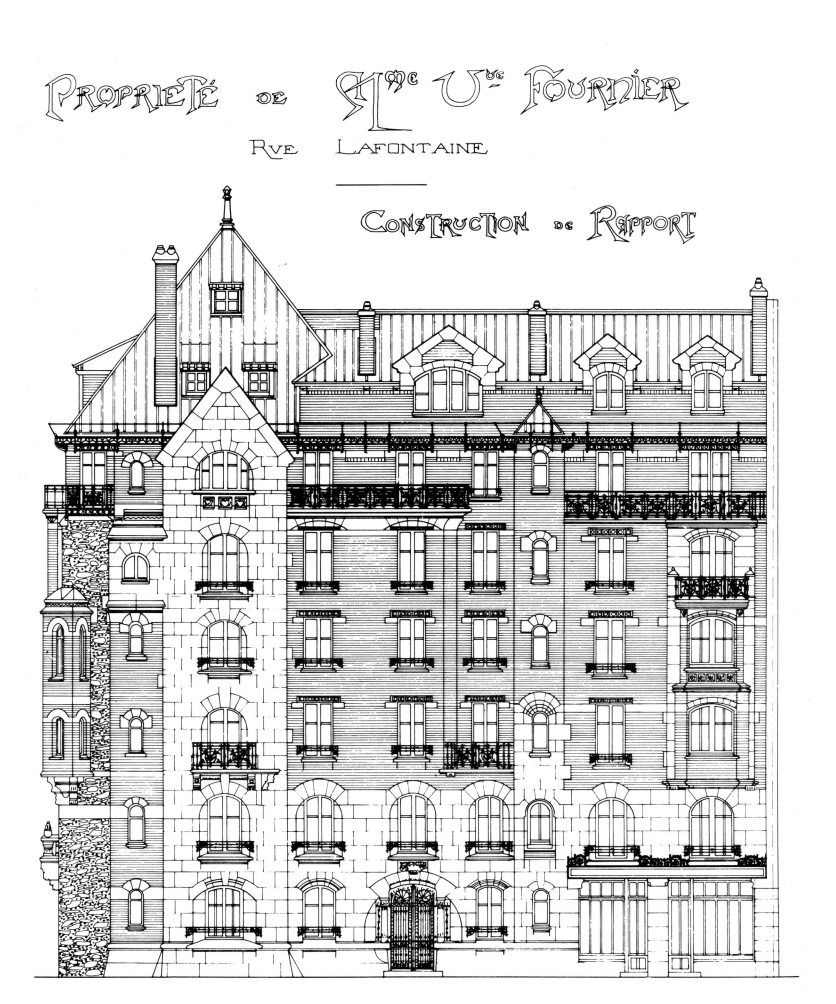

PROPRIÉTÉ DE Mme Vve FOURNIER

RUE LAFONTAINE

CONSTRUCTION DE RAPPORT

FAÇADE SUR LA RUE LAFONTAINE

The building opens with a grottolike vestibule, conceived in collaboration with the ceramist Alexandre Bigot, which functions as a kind of decompression chamber giving on both the exterior and interior. The decoration here is entirely based on the nervous serpentine line that would forever after mark the architect's style, and already at this early date it is decidedly abstract, a fact further emphasized by the glass bricks that give light to the stairwell.

Left: Vestibule window looking out on courtyard

Bottom left: Panel in enameled lava in the front hall

Bottom right: Cast-iron fountain in the courtyard. The original faucet is lost.

Opposite: Front hall

to break the monotony large bricked surfaces may create, the architect opened the cage of monsters and brought out sea horses that climb the height of the building, while the columns that give onto the "service" entrance discreetly recall the stylized phalluses delighted in by the statuaries of ancient Rome. In its form and singular appearance a fountain in the courtyard brings to mind those gigantic table centerpieces produced by the dynasty of the Germains, the renowned goldsmiths who worked for the last three kings of France under the old monarchy.

At the time everyone asked who would dare to live in a lair like that. Perhaps some eccentric born out of the imagination of a Huysmans. In those fireplaces, door bolts,

Vestibule and staircase

casement fastenings, locks designed by the master himself, people found only perversity: a home for the devil!

If a great many people were nonplussed by it all, the Castel nonetheless enchanted all those who would acquire a passion for Art Nouveau. Paul Signac, one of the greatest painters of the time and one of the Castel's first occupants, trumpeted his enthusiasm in an article in the *Revue Blanche* in 1899. To Félix Fénéon, one of the great seers of that epoch, he confided: "Do you know that in the house where we are going to have our nest—'Eccentric House' [in English] for the passersby but gay, practical, and bright for the tenants—there is even the telephone!" After moving in, the painter wrote to Fénéon: "Come soon, our blue staircase will amuse you."

Here we have examples of the stained-glass windows in what was Guimard's atelier on the ground floor. His graphic style was never more free and personal than in the stained glass and wallpaper he designed for the Castel Béranger. In those pure inventions, quite without reference to any definable object, his line developed without restraints, playing upon a few simple colors. Art Nouveau would never again attain such freedom, and if during the next fifteen years Guimard's imitators would copy what he did without acknowledging their debt, they would never achieve his nervous alertness of line and his limpidity of composition.

This page, clockwise from upper left: Guimard's worktable, in pearwood; The architect at his drawing table in his Castel Béranger studio. In the foreground, his pearwood worktable; A recent view of Guimard's onetime studio; Elevation of the courtyard façade of the main building

Opposite: The entrance from the second building into the courtyard

The side of the second building overlooking the Hameau

CASTEL BÉRANGER

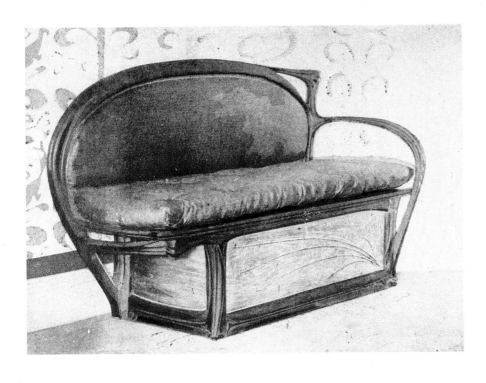

Pl. 50

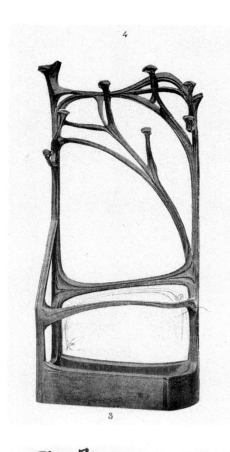

4

3

Pages 47–51: Illustrations from the album, *L'Art dans l'Habitation Moderne: Le Castel Béranger*, published by Guimard in 1898

Guimard did not care to publish or discuss his work, most often contenting himself with putting what he had to say into his constructions themselves. This makes the Castel Béranger album so much the more invaluable. A luxurious publication with hand-colored plates, it presents all of the architectural, decorative, and functional elements created especially for the building, including not only the furniture and stained-glass windows, but even the hardware and stoves. It makes a priceless catalogue of all of Guimard's production in his "first manner," a highly elaborate style that made no concessions and was marked by a nervousness his time must have found rather baffling. The impact remains no less today, if we judge by the combined wall bench and what-not case (see page 49, lower right) now in the Musée d'Orsay, Paris.

The album reports some of the public reactions to elements and objects that, like it or not, came with the apartments—stained glass, wallpaper, fireplaces, fittings—as well as certain optional creations, mostly furniture. Here, on our page 50, we have an exception to Guimard's otherwise designedly all-embracing art: a view of the interior decorator Pierre Selmersheim's atelier in Castel Béranger, furnished with the tenant's own creations.

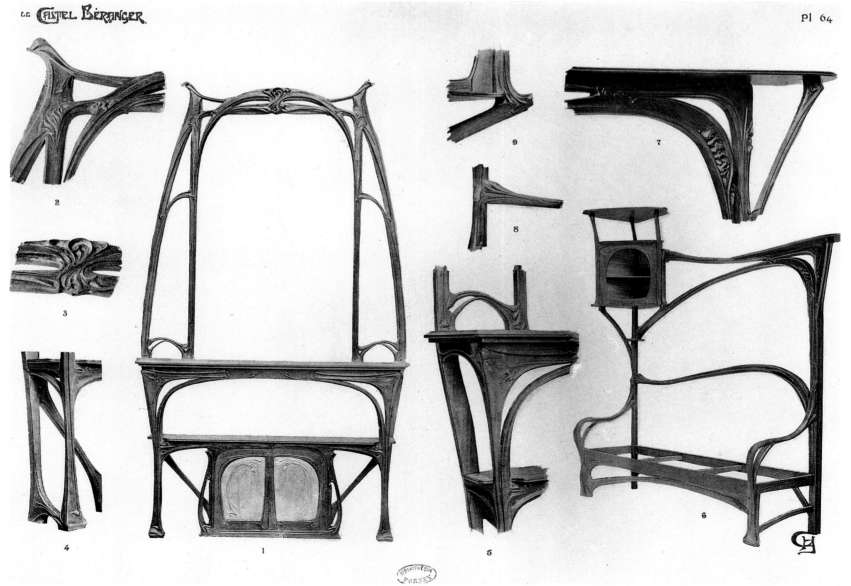

LE CASTEL BÉRANGER.

Pl 64

2

3

4

1

9

8

5

7

6

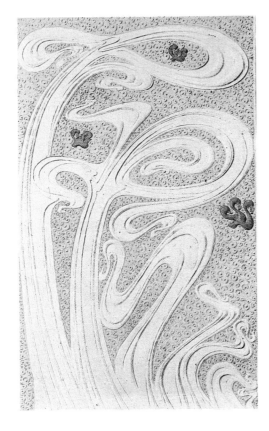
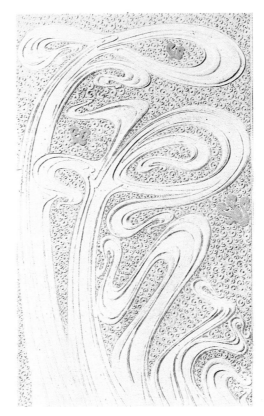

ECOLE DU SACRE COEUR

9 AVENUE DE LA FRILLÈRE

PARIS 16E

1895

Since the Middle Ages education has always played an important role in France, but except for the Sorbonne or the major religious institutions it was reserved for the children of privileged families and was very often carried out at home by a priest or tutor. Under the impulsion of Jules Ferry, instruction became public and obligatory. Whether staffed by laymen or the clergy, the school became the central point in the lives of children and adolescents. Perhaps it is because the idea of severity remains attached to the whole business of education that so many school buildings persist in dispensing with any touch of character, as if mediocrity favored the unfolding of young minds.

It was with the idea of giving education a better image that in 1895 the priests of Sacré-Coeur called on Guimard to build their new school. If the architect did not know from the start what he had to do, he had only to look at the façades and inner courts of the Parisian lycées—gloomy barracks for schoolboys—to learn what he ought not to do. By 1895 he was at the peak of his career. Resolutely modernist, here he had occasion to render homage to Joseph Vaudremer and Joseph Baudot, who were the first to think of opening wide windows in places of learning to let the sun pour in. Once again Guimard would seek ideas in the work of Viollet-le-Duc. The old master was the first to urge that forms should be subject to their initial function, and at the same time he recommended the use of metal and demonstrated how much more medieval art might have achieved if it had at its disposal iron, cast iron, and steel.

For this school building Guimard used lighter colored bricks than usual, combining beige with reddish tones. More than half the volume of the façade is taken up by windows which afford no end of light to the schoolrooms. Each is framed by uprights and supports in siliceous sandstone that are in their turn, on the lateral façades, separated by slender cast-iron colonnettes one scarcely notices. But the building's originality is in its base. In contrast to the usual slender elements, most often in cast iron, that prop up the roof of the covered walk around the playground, which is the pupils' only shelter in bad weather, Guimard distributed the mass of the school itself on a single cast-iron traverse girder which is itself supported by six struts set obliquely, rather like buttresses on medieval churches. That latter impression is reinforced by the fact that the cast-iron braces in which the supports rest are decorated with floral motifs that have something medieval about them, though here the flamboyant struts seem to function like pneumatic jacks that lift the entire building off the ground.

General view

This complex apparatus was to all intents and purposes described in Viollet-le-Duc's *Derniers Entretiens sur l'Architecture*, published around 1876, except that the old master planted the supports at right angles to the street while Guimard installed them at an angle and made them look more like props for a marquee than supports for a massive façade.

In the course of the last war the school had to close down. If the building escaped destruction it was thanks to its aesthetic qualities and its interest in terms of architectural technique. Leaving the building just as it was, the contractors converted portions into living quarters while maintaining the exterior intact, thus ensuring the survival of the building as a profitable income property.

Detail of a cast-iron supporting strut

The V-shaped arrangement of struts, inspired by Viollet-le-Duc

Opposite: Elevation of the main façade

While Guimard was hard at work on his Castel Béranger designs, he received a commission for a small religious educational complex comprising a school, a caretaker's house, and a building for the toilets. Erected in only a few months, the work was completed before it could incorporate anything of its architect's radical stylistic change of the moment. Nonetheless it shows his interest in functional decoration—the famous oblique columns—and a greater simplicity in laying out the façade.

ECOLE DU SACRÉ CŒUR

—— AVENUE DE LA FRILLIERE ——

BATIMENT DES CLASSES

ATELIER CARPEAUX

39 BOULEVARD EXELMANS
PARIS 16E

1895

A curious house, this. When the great sculptor's widow decided in 1895 to remodel her home, the master had been dead almost a quarter-century. She would create a pious mausoleum in memory of Carpeaux, who had created his statues in a modest atelier not far from there, at number 25 of the same boulevard. In deciding to have this work done, Madame Carpeaux was perhaps fulfilling the posthumous dream of a great artist who had always been the butt of criticism and, to his last day, had endured much misery on the material plane.

Entrusting Guimard with this task was in a way imagining what the encounter of those two spirits might have been like, enamored as both were of the baroque and above all of mannerism. Indeed, this elegant atelier seems more the thing for one of those painters or sculptors always sure to win a gold medal at the Salon and who could afford to live in an Asiatic opulence.

Since 1850 the more favored artists had often earned as much as their wealthiest clients. As new seigneurs in a prosperous society, their life-style was already comparable to that of certain great cultural overlords of our own century. A Meissonier, a Detaille, a Bonnat, a Bouguereau, each reserved his affection for the styles à la mode: Medieval, Renaissance, Louis XIII. It was in high-style retreats of the sort described by Balzac, Zola, and Anatole France that the painters held open house once a week. Just like the *grandes dames* of the time, they offered their visitors tea, and the clients got a look at the studio, previewed works in progress, and, seduced by the artist's savoir-faire, just couldn't wait to sit for him themselves.

The Carpeaux house façade is typically 1908–10 and has little in common with Guimard's usual style. Four-fifths of it is faced in freestone. The keynote is simplicity. There is no ironwork decoration, and the originality is confined to the upper floor with its large window opening. Light enters the atelier through eight windowpanes framed and topped by reddish bricks and a simple frieze. Two statues by Carpeaux ornament the façade.

Although the house is described as a work by Guimard, in reality it is not certain if he conceived it as a whole or only designed the upper story, the only one marked by his personality.

One of Carpeaux's sculptures ornamenting the façade

Carpeaux's heirs subjected the sculptor's studio on boulevard Exelmans to three successive transformations: in 1888 by Lewicki, in 1895 by Guimard (the only one to be commemorated by a signature on the façade), and in 1914 by Harant. Each architect's intervention was modest, and for Guimard it was chiefly a bread-and-butter matter. Yet one should not overlook the importance of such a commission within the web of personal relationships linking Guimard and his clients, at that particular moment the Catholic circles of Auteuil.

VILLA LA HUBLOTIERE

72 AVENUE DE MONTESSON
LE VÉSINET (YVELINES)

1896

Le Vésinet is some distance from Paris. Building land cost less; the architect could think big, giving free rein to his fantasy. Anyone who opted for Guimard knew what to expect. His work was anything but ordinary, and his Castel Béranger had become such an attraction that certain Sundays it was difficult to make your way up rue La Fontaine what with all the Parisians flocking to gaze at what a chronicler of the time dubbed "a lascivious monument." On the other hand, Guimard was said to do "psychological architecture": in each house he revealed a little of his client's character and personality. Reading *Remembrance of Things Past*—Proust, remember, was born in rue La Fontaine—it is easy to imagine the elegant Swann at home in the Carpeaux house, Dr. Cottard writing prescriptions in rue Agar, Odette in the flimsiest of attire trotting about in the hall of the Hôtel Mezzara.

As for this Villa La Hublotière, one cannot help wondering who was the responsive and courageous man who let Guimard have his way here. Perhaps a gentleman set on living with his time, a liberal perhaps. One can almost see Zola, Clemenceau, Jules Renard, Monet climbing the seven steps that lead to the front door on the side of the house.

Firmly planted on a solid mass of siliceous sandstone or granite, the house seems light and airy nonetheless. Access is through two arched vaults close to each other but with little in common. One sports a sort of cap; the other is much broader and stands free and therefore allows light to flood into the interior. The staircase is housed in a tower whose windows are set diagonally and speak clearly of what is behind them: an architectural exploit without equivalent unless, in more sketchy form and certainly with less elegance, in the courtyard of Castel Béranger.

Here the decoration is so perfectly integrated with the building that it takes a certain time to discern such beautiful touches as the fine carvings that frame the portal in contrast to the otherwise unadorned walls to either side of it. Such differences obey our master-architect's fundamental rule: in art nothing should be repetitive, beauty must never take the guise one expects.

Here again the old medievalist dream reappears in the motifs ornamenting the upper part of the door on the main front. And again ironwork expresses the architect's most personal traits. The graceful balconies, the play of the brackets supporting the guttering, the grilles along the peak of the roof are so many proofs of Guimard's genius.

The symmetry here may come as a surprise, but no doubt it should be read as Guimard's concern with fitting into an environment where superb villas adorned the little town then in full expansion and where "follies" and pastiches rose side by side. Perhaps too it was simply the prudence of a young architect who may well have realized that the Villa La Hublotière, being outside Paris, could not serve him as the kind of artistic manifesto he had created in the Castel Béranger and would soon make public in the Salle Humbert-de-Romans.

Basement windows

The main façade. Three salons open out to the terrace

The main doorway, on the side of the house

Out of sight of the passerby in the street, everything becomes much livelier. The rather aristocratic sobriety of the main façade gives place in the rear to a vast central mass with windows set obliquely to give full emphasis to the stairwell, here as always the central point of Guimard's constructions. In the terrace balustrades at the top of the house we have the only direct reference to Victor Horta, who had made such fluttering arabesques in wrought iron his personal hallmark and credo, though there is certainly no hint of pastiche here.

This middle-class villa—which takes its name from the hublots, the three portholelike ventilator openings on one of its façades—was Guimard's first undertaking to be entirely conceived after the innovations worked out in the Castel Béranger. There is the same fine and elegant workmanship in the stonecarving of the door recesses, in the ceramic plaques over the window openings, and in the astounding realizations in twisted wrought iron. While certain elements prepared for but not used in the Castel Béranger were reutilized in 1898–99 in the now-destroyed Hôtel Roy on boulevard Suchet in Paris and in the two pavilions of the Hameau Boileau (no longer recognizable), Guimard honored this important commission for a suburban villa by using only entirely new elements created for the occasion.

The rear façade

Vestibule

Side and rear of house from the garden

Detail of stone carving over the central door giving onto the terrace

Less eccentric than the entrance grille of the Castel Béranger, no doubt because of its symmetry, the garden gate of the villa is nonetheless closely related to its predecessor, an audacious marriage of tormented curves and straight lines that suddenly shoot off in unexpected directions. A work of art—yet created entirely out of standard industrial iron bars bent into surprising shapes.

The garden gate

SALLE HUMBERT-DE-ROMANS

60 RUE SAINT-DIDIER
PARIS 16E

1898
(Demolished, 1905)

In 1898 Père Lavy, a Dominican and a knowledgeable musicologist, succeeded in raising two million francs from friends of the order, with the idea of building what would be called today a cultural center. It would include a 1200-seat concert hall, an apartment for Père Lavy, and would accommodate the various activities of a religious house open to the faithful. Almost without opposition the ecclesiastical council decided to ask Guimard to take on the project. A difficult task, but here again Guimard saw a fine pretext for a display of his incomparable virtuosity.

The building has been demolished and is known only through its plans, some photographs, and a few written accounts, among them those by the architect Boileau and others by Fernand Mazade published at the time in a British review.

The main front on rue Saint-Didier overlooked a spacious courtyard set off from the street by an ornamental grille six and one-half feet high. The left-hand entrance gave onto the first vestibule, a vast space containing the cloakrooms, and there were two other vestibules spacious enough for uncrowded strolling.

The architect's ambition was to put up a building which would have the serious look proper to a religious institution, but without that crabbed and dismal air thought appropriate in those years to any place having to do with education and culture. Here we are already far from the Castel Béranger. For something like this, one needs to look at a number of buildings outside France, for instance the Whitechapel Art Gallery, which Townsend designed and built in the same period. Then too, certain details put one in mind of the extraordinary tea parlors Mackintosh designed in Glasgow in 1904.

To judge by the documents of the time, the interior decorations must have been astonishing: the ground-story flooring, for example, was made from a conglomerate simulating pink marble, inlaid with gilded motifs of lilies and water lilies. The stage comprised a platform large enough for an orchestra and, four steps higher, a vast area to accommodate a chorus. At the rear of the hall an imposing organ, whose mahogany case appears to have been conceived by Saint-Saëns himself, constituted a superb resounding wall.

The Humbert-de-Romans Auditorium was demolished in 1905 after a scant seven years. Who took the initiative to raze this extraordinary ensemble? It is said that the people in the neighborhood were glad of it, that they judged the building bizarre, diabolical even. No voice was raised in protest. The general conception, we are told, displeased the order, and in high places Père Lavy was considered as eccentric as the building erected through his efforts.

Opposite, above left:
Flyer advertising the Salle Humbert-de-Romans

Opposite, above right:
Ground plan of first floor

Opposite, below:
Elevation of the façade

The Humbert-de-Romans Auditorium, whose existence was of the briefest, inaugurated the era of Guimard's masterworks, works that would be playful, fantastic, even "edible" as Dali would have it. Of those key works, unfortunately, all too little survives. Guimard's apprentice years were over. The success of the Castel Béranger gave him reason for high hopes. The Humbert-de-Romans building, a major project, promised to be the occasion for a brilliant coup that would net him as much publicity as its predecessor. Nothing would be left to chance, down to every last detail. Certainly the architect was putting the organization that commissioned the building to ill-considered and risky expenses, but then again, he boasted, he was building with all possible economy (at least when it came to the basic materials). Unfortunately the undertaking got little attention (after all, a slightly eccentric concert hall virtually goes without saying), and its demolition caused so little stir that even the exact date is still uncertain. Its disappearance was not mourned in an out-of-the-way neighborhood which quite simply had no need for such a building.

(Dessin et Plan de M. GUIMARD, Architecte)

SALLE HUMBERT DE ROMANS
60, Rue Saint-Didier
LA PLUS BELLE SALLE DE CONCERT DE PARIS

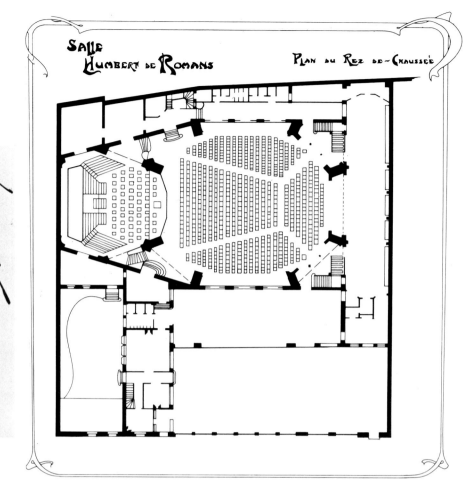

SALLE
HUMBERT DE ROMANS

PLAN DU REZ DE-CHAUSSÉE

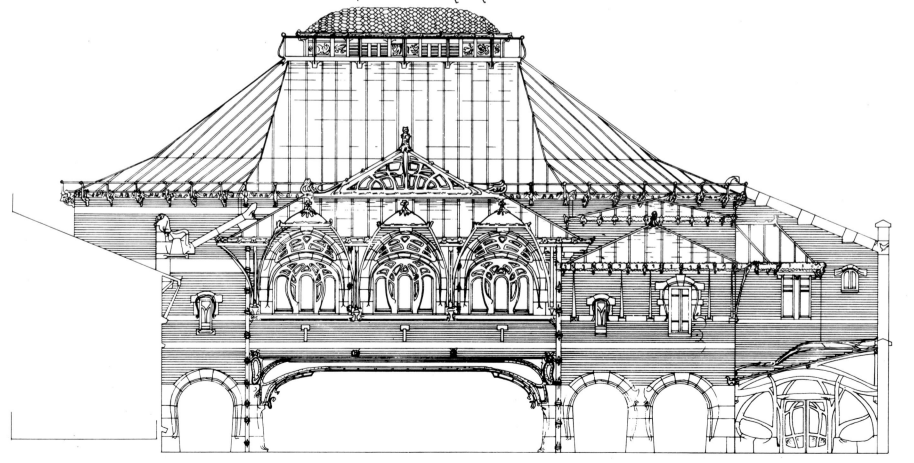

SOCIÉTÉ ANONYME IMMOBILIÈRE DE LA RUE SAINT-DIDIER CONSTRUCTION D'UNE SALLE DE MUSIQUE et PATRONAGE

FAÇADE PRINCIPALE SUR PRÉAU

MAISON COILLIOT

1898-1900

Athesis remains to be written on Guimard and ceramics. The architect of Castel Béranger was the first since the Renaissance to combine stone—often of the humblest sort, like siliceous sandstone—with ceramics of his own design which Eugène Gillet baked in his kilns. Nothing surprising then if he decided to make an absolute masterpiece of the shop and living quarters of a ceramics craftsman.

If you study the plans for the Coilliot house you expect to find everything asymmetrical. Yet the finished product strikes one as perfectly harmonious, rather like those architectural exploits so popular at the time among German architects, August Endell in particular.

Nothing here speaks of the past. Has anyone ever seen the main girder of a building utilized so as to distract the eye from a balcony, yet at the same time in a perfect position to support such an astonishing projecting roof? Or a building to all intents and purposes parallel to the street yet whose windows and rear form an angle of twenty degrees with the front? And the gaping covered loggia is like something out of a drawing by Gustave Doré.

One enters the shop with its spacious bays through a door that could have been vaulted by a Romanesque architect, which is surmounted by a striking motif reminiscent of an eye or, then again, a tear. The façade is faced with greenish turquoise ceramics produced by the proprietor himself.

The house strikes one as so much the more unusual for being situated in the outskirts of the city where none of the houses around it are more than two stories high.

A modest man indeed, this architect willing to work in an unassuming outlying neighborhood, as if he had done it all without the slightest thought of lucre, for the pure pleasure of it. And he made use here of line and curve with consummate skill. The letter C, used three times in a row in the shop sign, is at once admirable and witty, and the writing is very like that used on his Métro grilles to indicate the name of the station. What Guimard achieved here proves so much the more surprising to anyone who remarks the charming little neo-medieval house at 48 rue de Valmy, a few steps away, or the pseudo–Louis XV–Louis XVI hôtel at 177 boulevard de la Liberté: a lesson in the distance that separates genius from honest know-how.

One can imagine the astonishment of the good folk of Lille when the hoardings came down and gave them their first glimpse of this building.

Air vents

Ceramic shop sign

Vestibule

Façade on the street

Long before Le Corbusier and his "maison du fada" (the Cité Radieuse in Marseille), Guimard had the privilege of erecting in Lille what some locals still refer to as "the crazy house," an asymmetrical construction of Gothic inspiration, but a Flemish-style Gothic such as he surely saw on his visit to Belgium. With utter virtuosity he made light of all the difficulties he set himself: the interlocking of empty spaces and solid structures, a façade composed out of a complexity of planes, and, not least, a vivid use of color. The latter was obtained by applying over the entire outside wall a coat of fluid lava, either enameled or reconstituted (something possible because the material could be molded and thus made adaptable to all the subtleties of Guimard's linear decoration) according to a procedure perfected by the Gillets, father and son, both expert ceramists. To my knowledge this is the only instance of such extensive use of lava on a single construction. Treated like a facing substance with the same validity as brick or tiles, it is one more proof of Guimard's curiosity about all the problems and possibilities of materials.

Air vents

Front hall

VILLA LA BLUETTE

Cartouche near the front door

Looking at the front of this villa Guimard built at the turn of the century one may well wonder what Vitruvius and Palladio, architects of earlier times, who have always been thought of as exemplars of rigor and harmony, might have thought of this work. Perhaps they would have ascribed its fantastic look to the pranks of a god of the winds who, having swept in through an open window, had literally blown the house about from inside, swelling it here and there without demolishing it. The apparent disharmony of the façades, underscored by a subtle play of planes, is utterly novel. The second story, with its graceful balcony held up by slender wooden brackets, brings to mind nothing less than swirls and folds of cloth. The overall airiness of this balcony is counterbalanced by the mass of small stones that enclose the window at the right, like a precious mount for a fine gem.

Thanks to a system of support utilizing inclined girders rising from the ground, the part of the house that projects on the left is brought back into equilibrium, and the general idea recalls the astonishing experiment Guimard had carried through in the Ecole de Sacré-Coeur in Paris.

Disharmony perhaps, but as always the architect took pleasure in throwing all the classical rules into question, as the four windows on the ground story testify. The height of wit and irony, a magician's sleight of hand, those four openings appear exactly right only when one notices the fifth window on the circular tower at the right.

Under a roof that looks as though it had been made in Kyoto, the architect played with his materials. On the rear façade, to the left, the small stones stacked one on top of the other recall a river whose calm surface is gently disturbed by a crosswind, while to the right, the architect uses the play of light to create a surface of large pieces of sandstone that evokes an avalanche released by a melting glacier. This façade includes nine openings scattered like dead leaves in autumn in a meadow. Each one is a small masterpiece of grace, of originality; only one appears more assertive—functional, as one would say today—the back door.

The front door—one might call it a dragonfly as seen by a classical painter—bats its wings; it would very much like to fly. This section of the house, although a bit too classical, is enlivened by an inscribed cartouche. Here the surprising color and design are reminiscent of Guimard's work in the rue Agar in Paris, and in Lille. The entrance to the villa reveals how important the medieval universe was to the architect. The

(continued on page 78)

At the very time Guimard was busy working out his plans for the Paris Métro, he designed most of his famous and most eccentric villas: the Modern Castel in Garches (now transformed), the Castel Henriette in Sèvres (destroyed), and the Villa La Bluette at Hermanville, which has been preserved practically without change.

Since the house is situated on a stretch of Normandy coast, the architect did not hesitate to make use of half-timbering, shingle (from the beach at Etretat), and, of all things, shells. All the parts in wood were painted blue, whence the villa's name; and all that eye-catching color scarcely made it an inconspicuous seaside retreat.

An inveterate partisan of a total art, Guimard also designed the furniture, the strange fireplace in the living room, and even the enclosing wall along the sea.

The house lost its name at an unknown date. The wooden fence along the street now carries the name "La Houle" (The Sea Swell). It is not impossible that that new name goes back even to Guimard's time, perhaps because the house soon changed hands. Postcard views show that minor modifications were made very early.

The main façade overlooking the sea

The main entrance

Details of the rear façade

roundness of the granite blocks, particularly those above the seven steps, cannot fail to evoke the Coilliot house in Lille. Finally, a tender detail: the use, for the first time in decor, of shells, which almost seem to have been collected by a child at the shore.

The fireplace, a sumptuous centerpiece, is the principal ornament of the large living room. It must be accounted a masterpiece both as a typical "Object 1900" and, at the same time, because it is integrated so well into the room. Its stylistic origins in Lorraine, and even the Nancy of Emile Gallé, are emphasized by the way it evokes the stoves so much in use in the past centuries in Lorraine, Alsace, and Germany. More than just a fireplace, it is a piece of furniture that seems to have ignited from its own heat: flame motifs curl around the bases of the three shelves, and the flamelike forms of the floral ornament at the top threaten the ceiling.

View of the rear façade

The living room, with a view of the sea

The fireplace

VILLA LA SAPINIERE

1899

At first sight one is struck by a certain maritime look in Guimard's constructions. Here, a dreamer like myself would think of those wooden superstruc-
tures—"castles"—which in days of yore crowned sailing ships riding high in
the water, something that will be even more striking, and stranger, in the roof of the
Villa Hemsy.

As a building or, better, an "architectural object," the Villa La Sapinière is
calmer than its neighbor, the Villa La Bluette. Quite the opposite, too, of such splen-
did residences as the Castel Béranger or the Hôtel Guimard. La Sapinière affects a
certain show of timidity in the way its concave parts draw back, recoil even, and to this
its numerous doors add an element of mystery.

Apart from the concavity of its front and the way its roof seems to flap over, this
villa strikes one as among the most classical Guimard built: there is already a hint of
the house he would build in 1905 in Eaubonne. The wooden panels lacquered white
on its façades may be a homage to the decorators of the Secession in Vienna, who were
making great use of wood painted in pale colors—unless one wishes to view those
panels as sails for the convoy that would set forth around 1920 flying the banner of Art
Déco.

*The date of this villa (now divided into apart-
ments) is not known. Although it is situated
only a little over one-eighth of a mile from La
Bluette, it is difficult to think of the two villas
as contemporaries. La Sapinière seems closer
to the Villa La Surprise in Cabourg, dated
1902–03, which was destroyed in the last war.*

*The present villa is an unfortunate illustration
of how changes in taste have been fatal to Guimard's conceptions, altering their nature beyond recovery. The building remains, but its
chief originality disappeared with the removal
of the second-story terrace supported on broad
wooden arches and making a covered porch on
the ground floor. As often, here Guimard exploited circular forms emerging from a void,
which gives them a light and airy, almost ethe-
real look. Little survives of the original balconies and windows. La Sapinière is no more
than a phantom, with its basic forms mutilated
no less than its decoration.*

Postcard showing the building in its
original state

General view

METROPOLITAIN

1900

The adventures and misadventures of the Paris Métro are very much a part of the "little history" of the great city. Just getting about had been something like a nightmare before the Métro was built. A glance at photographs and postcards from before the turn of the century is enough to tell us what disorder reigned in the streets of Paris: it may even have been more anarchical than what we have to put up with today. Going on foot was as difficult as it was dangerous in the perpetual war between pedestrians, horse-drawn vehicles, omnibuses, and fiacres.

Not that public transport was something new. The Parisians had been practicing it for centuries, ever since Blaise Pascal organized carriages with a five-sous fare, ancestors of our shared taxis.

Not before 1828, however, were there omnibuses. In 1855, for thirty centimes inside and fifteen outside, you could cross the length of Paris. (Stable currency, the French: the tariff was still the same in 1905.)

But from day to day Paris was becoming more bottlenecked. In the City Council the idea was raised of a railroad that would serve each quarter. There was much debate about whether the trains should run on the surface or underground. The latter idea was attractive, but the old lobby of people catering to transportation had a loud voice: to hear them, those railroad-type carriages into which hundreds of people would be jammed would bring on the world the seven plagues of Egypt. Cholera! Fevers! And what about safety, the bugbear they came back to again and again? The modernists retorted that underground networks existed and flourished throughout the Western world: in London since 1863, in Berlin since 1871, in New York since 1872, and now Vienna was claiming to have the finest subway system in the world.

Progress will have its way. By 1895, the projects for the 1900 Exposition Universelle were already drawn up, completed. In two years the President of the Republic would inaugurate the worksite. The reports of the Prefects and the Minister of the Interior were categorical: if things remained as they were, within a few days of the opening of the fair it would be impossible to move a step in the capital. Finally, in 1896, the Compagnie Générale des Transports was granted the concession. Their contract specified the construction of six lines with a total length of seventy kilometers. Fulgence Bienvenüe, a young graduate of the Ecole Polytechnique who taught mathematics to Charles de Foucauld, would carry the undertaking through to the end. Everything was ready in time for the Exposition; visitors were enthusiastic, and people took the Métro as in our times they visit Disneyland or the Centre Pompidou.

I knew that first specimen of Métro: I took it every morning at "Jasmin" and got out at "Pompe." Since then it has gone from success to success. The carriages that used to make as much noise as the Creusot dump trucks have been replaced by cars more silent than the Orient Express, and just as speedy: to go from the avenue de New-York to "Argentine" it takes less time than . . . in twenty years the space shuttle will need to link New York with Buenos Aires.

If Guimard's name is on the lips of all those enamored of Art Nouveau, to most people it would be as good as unknown were it not that it brings to mind the entrances to the Métro.

(continued on page 88)

Enameled iron panel, Porte Dauphine

The Porte Dauphine station at the entrance to the Bois de Boulogne.

For more than fifteen years people in high places had been worrying about those entrances, about what their gates would look like: outward displays to hide the shabbiness underneath, as one editorialist of the time described them. As early as 1890, dossiers on the subject began to pass through the hands of Charles Garnier, the masterful builder of the Opéra who was then president of the Société Centrale des Architectes, a sort of super-Académie that lorded it over the profession.

Many people despised those modernists who, among other misdeeds, had erected the Eiffel Tower. For lovers of the past, if one had to put up with an underground railroad it should at least be made as discreet as possible. Garnier warned the minister of public works that, as he saw it, the entrances should in no manner have an industrial character. Each should be sumptuous, signaled by columns carved in the antique manner and in bronze, granite, onyx.

It took the intervention of the finger of fate, and a decision pushed through by a functionary whose name deserves to grace a Métro station, before Guimard's proposals (repeatedly modified) finally won out.

Guimard turned his designs over to the Fonderie de Saint-Dizier, a foundry which for years would hold the monopoly of "artistic castings for buildings, fireplaces, articles for gardens and cemeteries in Style Guimard." The architect chose cast iron because it lends itself easily to the curves that were his hallmark. The supple and well-rounded modeling produced by casting, which rules out spikes and too-sharp forms, would accentuate the volumes of those small Métro entrances, making them appear more important. Thus, thanks to the genius of a creative artist, an ordinary metal would prove the perfect stuff for utilitarian monuments of particularly elegant appearance. Each entrance would be treated in accord with the character of the station: here mascarons, there struts in the form of branching stems or the musculature of a creature from another world, while a lamp, a beacon concealed within a large corolla, would shine like an eye behind half-closed lids.

So many singularities, so much charm put at the service of the Parisians, could not help but fascinate Dali, who would speak of "those divine entrances to the Métro, by grace of which one can descend into the region of the subconscious of the living and monarchical aesthetic of tomorrow."

At about the same time, around 1898, Otto Wagner designed a project for a station of the Vienna subway. Overall successful, it is perhaps a little too pretty, and in any case less revolutionary that the Dauphine or Bastille stations in Paris.

At first Guimard's grilles bothered people but most often they were laughed at. On the eve of World War II there was the threat of an order from the Prefect authorizing the wreckers to destroy the cast-iron monuments now so very out of date. However, when a great collector installed one in his private park, and the Museum of Modern Art in New York rushed to acquire the Bastille station, a masterpiece in its genre, some people had second thoughts, especially since with time Guimard's arabesques were coming to seem even more amazing: add the charm of yesteryear to the beauty already there and each of those grilles becomes a ravishing object in itself.

Now, in our time, if some minister were to get the idea of touching a single one of the survivors, he would run the risk of having his head chopped off by public opinion and set up as an ornament on the Danton station.

Guimard was awarded the contract for the Paris Métro entrances even though he did not take part in the open competition. The attempt has often been made to justify this bit of hanky-panky with purely artistic arguments. But it is hardly likely that Guimard's reputation or the radical newness of his art, which, in point of fact, was often viewed at the time as an offence to good taste, had much bearing on his selection.

The construction of the Métro entrances was a major operation. It involved erecting hundreds of small shelters in the most important streets of the capital and in proximity to the most renowned monuments. What the candidates for this lucrative commission submitted turned out to be, invariably, massy little stone buildings which were more or less successful pastiches. But what really mattered was that they took up too much room and were designed with not a thought for the narrowness of the sidewalks or for other structures in the immediate vicinity. With his clever invention of a horizontal name-plate, which was visible from a distance and could be lighted at night, Guimard stood out head and shoulders above the rest, while the structures he designed, without any jarring and encumbering opaque walls, fitted easily into any and every site in the city.

Since the underground network had been conceived in its entirety almost from the start (so as to block the city with worksites only once), it was immediately clear how many station entrances would be required and what special problems certain of them might pose. Because Guimard's procedure was based on a system of standardized industrial elements that could be repeated in the same forms and in all sizes, it guaranteed adaptability to all possible circumstances. Cast iron moreover was decidedly more economical and easier to manipulate than stone.

The inauguration of the subway system was scheduled to coincide with the Exposition Universelle of 1900. The first line, which ran from Porte Maillot to Porte de Vincennes, was inevitably thought of as something of prime importance, a kind of triumphal main route, whence the idea of erecting real stations here and there or, at any rate, more imposing shelters. For this, at key spots on the line, Guimard placed differently designed structures ranging from a simple enclosure to a full-scale station (Etoile, Bastille), with here and there an intermediary type known today as the "dragonfly" because of its glass roof, whose projecting panes recall the insect's wings (Hôtel de Ville, now shifted to the Abbesses station). On the walls of the latter two types there were panels in reconstituted lava manufactured by Eugène

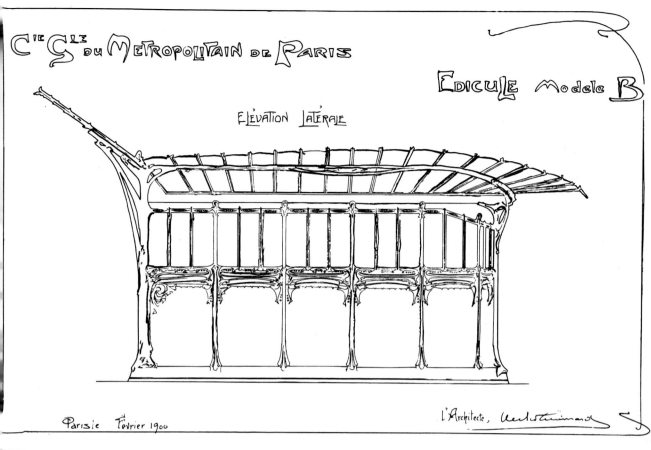

Cie G^{le} du Metropolitain de Paris

Edicule Modele B

Elévation Latérale

Paris le Février 1900

L'Architecte, Hector Guimard

Gillet, who at the same time was turning out elements for the Coilliot house in Lille, then under construction.

Guimard's shelters were to be sited along the entire span of the network. But his collaboration with the company in charge came to an end in 1904 when it was decided to dispense with more of his creations: it seemed unthinkable to tolerate one of those strange enclosures in front of the sumptuous Palais Garnier, at "Opéra."

Guimard's drawings for the type-B shelter, Porte Dauphine station

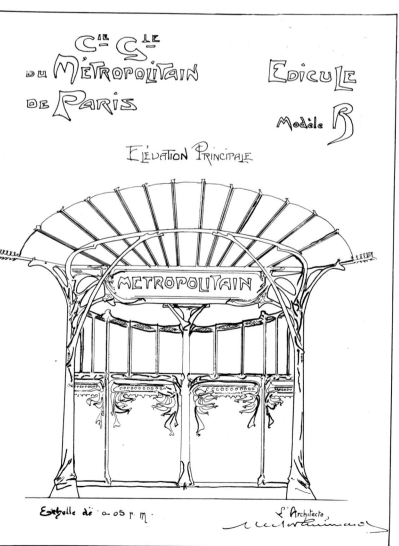

Cie G^{le} du Métropolitain de Paris

Edicule Modèle B

Elévation Principale

METROPOLITAIN

Echelle de 0.05 p. m.

L'Architecte, Hector Guimard

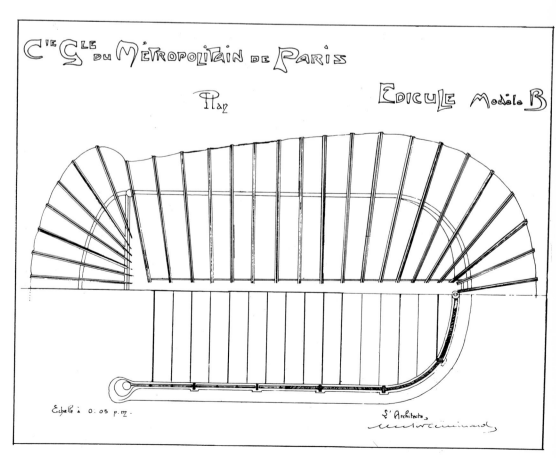

Cie G^{le} du Métropolitain de Paris

Plan

Edicule Modèle B

Echelle à 0.05 p. m.

L'Architecte, Hector Guimard

Detail of the Abbesses station

Side view of the Porte Dauphine station at the Bois de Boulogne

The Abbesses station in Montmartre

63. — *Paris*. - Stations du Métropolitain. - Place de l'Etoile.

P. Marmuse, Paris.

Postcard of the place de l'Etoile station

Detail of a drawing by Guimard
of a support for a station sign

Postcard of the Bastille station

173. - PARIS. - Une Gare du Métropolitain (Bastille)

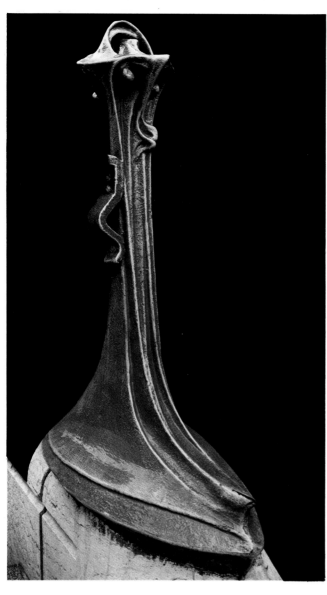

Ironwork for stations, including a lamp (*above*), and various handrails.

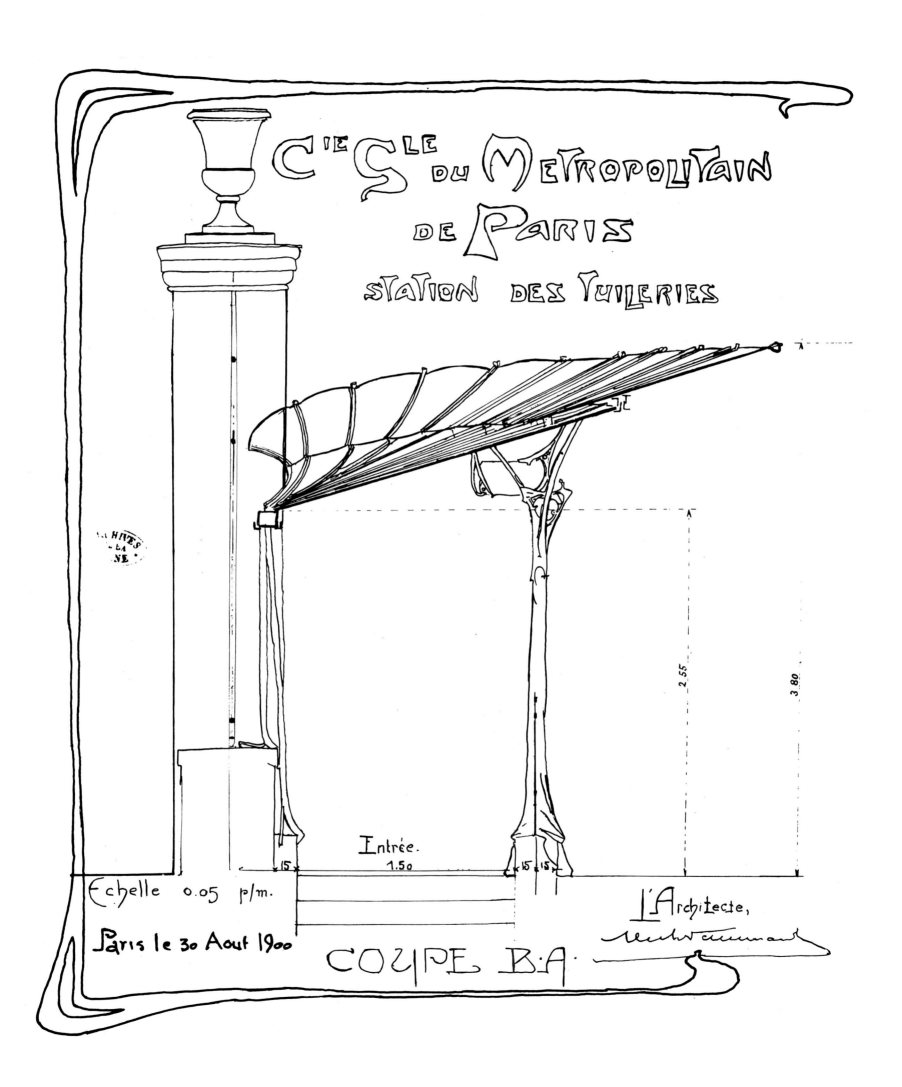

Cie Gle du Métropolitain
de Paris
Station des Tuileries

2.55

3.80

Intrée.
1.50

15   15 15

Echelle   0.05   p/m.

Paris le 30 Aout 1900

COUPE B.A.

L'Architecte,

Plans of the Tuileries station

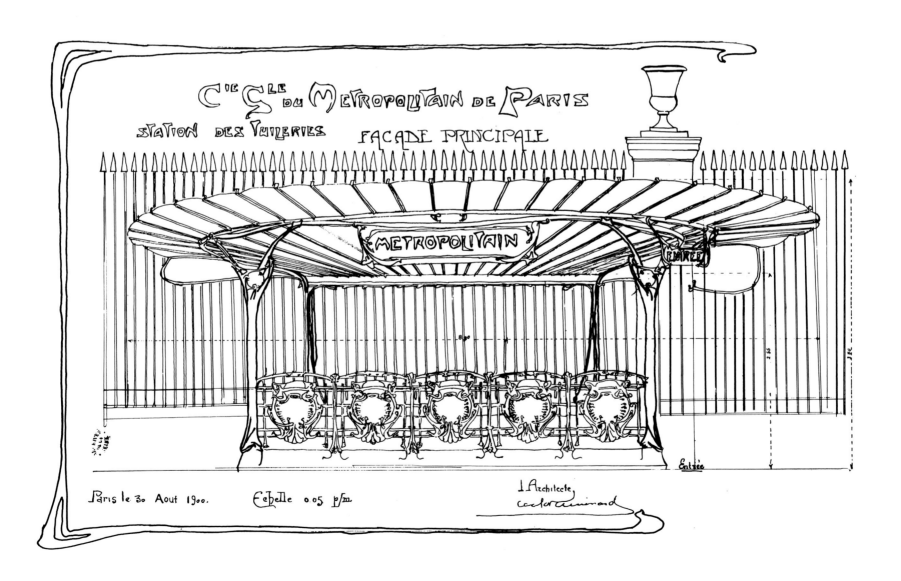

Lamp holder

Detail of a handrail

Place Blanche station

CASTEL VAL

1903

Unlike other residences Guimard built outside Paris, the Castel Val is like an enormous natural bubble—a pearl—resting lightly on the ground. Here, contrary to Guimard's usual practice, no architectural element projects, neither the ground floor opened up by large bays that give onto what one takes to be reception rooms, nor the second story with its two simple windows on the façade. The originality of it all becomes clear on the house's flanks, of which one has a covered balcony and the other a semicircular gallery. Only the right-hand part of the façade can be considered altogether typical of Guimard, with its door decorated with ironwork tracery and the cast-iron pillar propping up the second story. Apart from the metal supports, the house is built entirely in siliceous sandstone and bricks in two colors.

Next to the last of Guimard's "castels"—witnesses to a brilliant epoch when he played with brio the role of a Parisian celebrity who could do almost everything he fancied—the Castel Val reveals not so much a style running out of breath as a change in method. Up to and including the Villa La Bluette, artists like Müller, Bigot, or Gillet had collaborated with Guimard, supplying ceramic or lava decorations for his buildings. Sculptors too at times— Guérin at the Hôtel Delfau, Ringel d'Illzach at Castel Béranger—had had their part in the carved decoration of his façades. But the pavilion in "Style Guimard" at the Exposition de l'Habitation at Paris in 1903 would be their last effort in common, at one and the same time homage and farewell. Thenceforth, absolute master of every line and every volume, Guimard would refuse such decorative artifices: he would design every last item and entrust the realization only to technicians working directly under his authority.

The fundamental form of this house, coiling around itself like a snail shell, suffices to ensure a consistent unity. Since 1902 the architect had been working for the Nozal family, and the Castel Val was built for a friend of theirs. The Nozals were industrialists who would soon become Guimard's chief source of commissions and his associates in real estate developments. His architecture was changing, attuning itself to a new group of clients.

Entrance

Overleaf: General view

JASSEDE APARTMENTS

142 AVENUE DE VERSAILLES—
1 RUE LANCRET
PARIS 16E

1903

In Paris, as early as the end of the seventeenth century, buildings were already erected purely as income property, with apartments rented out. They were strictly human rabbit warrens, and as in modern tenements there was no thought of decoration, but only of the minimum necessities for housing a fraction of the population that fortune had not favored. Not before the start of our century was there indoor plumbing.

After 1850, however, the large cities began to appoint commissions to ensure that certain urban ensembles would be respected. In Paris an effort would be made to harmonize the large thoroughfares, the boulevards Haussmann, Malesherbes, Péreire and, a little later, avenue Henri-Martin.

Young sculptors with diploma in hand were called in to decorate apartment building façades. Buildings began to be "signed." Property owners wished to be considered aesthetes. Even Rodin in his first years decorated house fronts. Likewise, more attention was given to vestibules and staircases, and they were treated with as much concern as in private dwellings.

All of which cost money and meant higher rents, but tenants in those buildings didn't mind as long as their homes gave visible proof of their fortune and good taste.

At the dawn of Art Nouveau, beginning in 1895, a certain number of capitalists claiming to be avant-garde commissioned architects still unknown to the general public. That was how Guimard started out and prospered, and within the perimeter of Auteuil and Passy he would eventually build ten or so apartment buildings, among them these Jassedé Apartments. With a vast terrain—delimited by the avenue de Versailles and rue Lancret—at his command, the architect could face his task with a light heart. What he produced here, with its structure, materials, and massive use of brick, has no need of an architect's signature: it is pure Guimard.

On the side toward the Seine, as well as on that giving on rue Lancret, a series of bow windows, each of a different volume, give breadth to the ensemble. The projecting windows give the occupants on the avenue de Versailles side a view of the river across the way, but also of the spectacle of the street. On rue Lancret, at a distance from the quai, the solution is banal, with corner balconies opening off less important rooms and service rooms.

Guimard is brilliant in his manner of arranging balconies, like the one on the third story that sweeps around the façade like a girdle, or the platform on the fourth story placed at an angle and off-axis with respect to the bow window that projects above it. This bow window is itself roofed by a terrace fenced off from the void by no more than a simple and delightful flourish of ironwork. Equally noteworthy, the small "maids' rooms" on the topmost story are each covered by a sort of quaint capping, once again a wink at the would-be medieval style.

(continued on page 106)

Front door

The main front is built in beige-colored bricks of two different tones, varied here and there by elements of a more russet tinge. The main door is imposing, rather like one on a Romanesque edifice that had got its final decoration at the start of the Flamboyant Gothic. The decoration of the vestibule off the avenue de Versailles is audacious, stripped to essentials, and so too the floral banister of the staircase and the pilasters that buttress the building. Blond wood is used to contrast with metallic elements painted gray.

Nothing escaped the architect's vigilant eye, neither the door fittings, the locks, nor the wrought-iron doors. The grillwork is sometimes all in straight lines, sometimes sinuous and floral. The architect amused himself by adding touches borrowed from the Orient to a building that is otherwise quite medieval.

Elevation of the façade
on the "Cour des Miracles"

Vestibule

General view

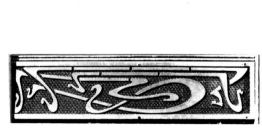

Detail of a balcony

Balconies on the façade

Façade on the avenue de Versailles

Service doorway on the rue Lancret

While engaged with an important series of villas and "castles" in country places, Guimard returned to Paris to put up two adjoining buildings for an old crony, Louis Jassedé. They would be his only such buildings in this prosperous period, and for good reason: the opened-out and broken-up volumes he favored could be realized to the full only in a garden setting, away from the constraints of the Parisian building authorities who kept strict control over anything that might jut out in new buildings. Here, however, at the corner of avenue de Versailles and rue Lancret he could give free rein to a play of curving balconies that are not aligned with each other and that create a highly successful though decidedly singular overall animation.

Detail is by and large limited to delicately sculpted decorative elements and an exquisitely worked ensemble of cast-metal fittings, the first products of a series of "artistic castings" designed for commercial exploitation in collaboration with a foundry at Saint-Dizier.

Inside door to the vestibule

The architect's signature

Air vent and coal chute opening

Twinned windows on the ground floor,
rue Lancret

Air vent

Detail of a doorjamb

HOTEL NOZAL

52 RUE RANELAGH
PARIS 16E

1904
(Demolished, 1957)

Who can define fashion and taste, who can tell their limits and point a finger at their perversities?

When the Hôtel Nozal rose before their eyes, the Parisians were struck with admiration: yet another sign of Guimard's genius—and of the aesthetic daring of the house's owner. But luck was against it. Two years before the work was completed, Monsieur Nozal was killed in an automobile accident. His wife, however, faithful to what he had had in mind, begged Guimard to go ahead.

Only fifteen years later, what had shown itself a short time before to be as beautiful as it was striking now looked uncouth, distressingly old-fashioned. Its forms were laughed at; they lacked spine and substance. The building was as flabby as Dali's soft watches, a cake whose sugar icing had sat too long in the sun.

In 1945 a bomb could have done the job, but it wasn't until 1957 that the Hôtel Nozal was delivered over to the wreckers, a victim of the great real estate boom. On its site would rise a profitable apartment house. Luck was not with the Hôtel Nozal. In 1970 the Commission for Historical Monuments would have cried a halt to its destruction, and in 1984 the photographer and the author of this book would have been able to prowl amazedly all around the house before extolling its strange beauty; by 2050 it would have been impossible to push one's way through the rue de Ranelagh for the Japanese pouring out of their tourist buses with camera at the ready.

There were other works already under construction, but the year 1904 would be largely devoted to creating a ravishing "palace" for Léon Nozal, his new patron. The mansion, alas, was destroyed, but by chance part of its furnishings were donated to the Musée des Arts Décoratifs in Paris. Everything about it was totally new and of a staggering luxuriousness. There Guimard exercised without reserve his taste for nervous curves, steep pitched roofs, elegant ironwork. He had probably not had such a free hand since Castel Béranger and the Salle Humbert-de-Romans.

Façade elevation in photograph and architect's drawing

CASTEL D'ORGEVAL

1904

The Castel d'Orgeval is something out of a surreal dream: the sublimation of all the houses Guimard invented, a Samurai warrior's armor, a military headquarters that would have sent some Gustave Doré rushing for his pen. My grandson to whom I showed the photographs of the Castel assured me that it was in this château of strange shadows that Skeletor went through his gymnastics before sallying out to do battle with He-Man.

Everything here is of an extreme gracefulness, and the originality of the volumes makes it one of the most successful of all Guimard's works. The main front with its broad conical roof projecting over it brings to mind some mysterious periscope which, like the fox's eye, can take in everything within a span of 180 degrees.

The bulk of the building is of rough-cut blocks, which are interrupted by areas of the light-colored brick used for the tower. Guimard's way of playing with his materials here is virtually diabolical, so well did he succeed in combining sandstone with brick. Stone he brought to the fore, to the front line as it were, whereas brick, his favorite, was kept safe in the rear ranks, sometimes sheltered under the overhanging roof of the door, elsewhere finding refuge in stretches that matter less.

As in the Chalet Blanc in Sceaux, wood plays an important role here. By its nature, by its supple and simple forms, it combines marvelously well with masonry and helps to dispel the disturbing note the "castle" might otherwise convey. The rear façade is rather more orderly, or would be, except that on the left side of the building the architect contrived not only to combine sandstone and brick, but succeeded in imposing a brick shape recalling a lighter-than-air balloon in the stone.

Asymmetry reigns throughout, but never at the expense of harmony.

Every fruitful period in an artist's life ought to be capped with a masterpiece. Although the Hôtel Nozal was delivered over to the wreckers, we can still marvel at the Castel d'Orgeval, the strange last "castle" Guimard would build. The very idea of a façade has been discarded, and the four faces of the building simply interpenetrate. Built in siliceous sandstone, brick, and wood, the house has the ornamental simplicity proper to a country dwelling. One cannot praise too highly the sheer inventiveness of the forms. Here Guimard summed up ten years of his career: a tower recalling that of the Castel Henriette, commodious wooden balconies decorated as in the Villa La Surprise but forming something like a bridge projecting over a large empty space as in La Sapinière, a side door like that in the Hôtel Roy, curving walls as in the Castel Val, and the triangular dormer windows seen in his works several times since the Ecole du Sacré-Coeur.

This house had a difficult history. Its construction went very slowly—two years—and its final appearance was quite unlike what was planned. After the end of 1904 Guimard did a great deal of designing but built little until 1909, the year of his marriage. In the intervening four years the only important commissions he received were for the development of the park around the Castel d'Orgeval, this private dwelling, and the Chalet Blanc in Sceaux. Without speaking of poverty, one can imagine that he went through a trying time that must have given him food for thought and induced him to curb his difficult character.

While preparing the models for cast-metal objects to be manufactured at Saint-Dizier and carrying through a few decorating projects, Guimard was learning also to restrain his customary fever of invention, and this hôtel is the first example of a new approach.

Detail of the façade

The front door

View from the side

Ground-floor window

Garden façade

General view of the main façade

HOTEL DERON-LEVENT

1905

To have one's own hôtel in Paris has been, since the mid-nineteenth century, the mark of those who had "made it." The elegant and cultivated among the bourgeoisie were always on the lookout for places to live once occupied by princes or potentates, but most of the heroes of Balzac or Zola—bankers, courtesans, newspaper tycoons—had houses built especially for them which were more modest but nonetheless left no one in doubt of their occupant's financial status.

As well-heeled as they were, they could afford to engage architects to put up residences marked by an opulent elegance. Inclined to a passion for a long-past world, egged on by the literature so fashionable at the time, like the heroes of Dumas or Ponson du Terrail or Eugène Sue, their one ambition was to live in a properly medieval, Renaissance, or Louis XIII decor. That chilliness toward things of their own time, that refusal of everything modern, was the start of a veritable drying up of the creative idea. Hugo stigmatized such decadence; Alphonse Karr attacked the system, and in particular the official teachings. His article, written in the middle of the last century, could be countersigned by an observer of our day: "An architect learns during ten years to make Greek temples—and ends up having his hands full building apartments to rent at 500 francs under the direction of a chief foreman. . . . His most sublime inventions are confined to the all too few different combinations that can be made with five capitals of columns which, moreover, make a dreadful effect when mixed together." Nor did Huysmans go at it with a light hand when he proclaimed that, "they are finished, the architects; people who trick themselves out with that name are yokels, bricklayers devoid of all personality, all science." Which means that one really has to applaud the courage of such people as the Deron-Levents who, at the turn of the century, did not hesitate to turn to Guimard when it came to building their house.

We are in 1907, and the Hôtel Deron-Levent is completed. Some time has passed since the Castel Béranger went up. Art Nouveau is beginning to strike some people as passé, whence Guimard's more prudent approach.

The Hôtel Deron-Levent is half-hidden by the Hôtel Jassedé. Its typically Guimardesque façade consists of two joined structures, one flat-surfaced and capped by a projecting peaked roof, the other intended primarily for receiving guests, with two large bays. Contrary to Guimard's usual practice, and perhaps because of the narrowness of the lot here, although the six windows are each different, they are nonetheless placed symmetrically. The beige and gray tones of the brick go nicely with the tonalities of the stone trimmings. Decoration is reduced to a minimum: a few swirls of carved stone that serve as consoles to support the balconies. As usual, however, wrought-iron elements are treated in a remarkable manner. Thus the gutter across the upper story at the left is held up by a slender iron apparatus made to look like a torch holder that might illuminate part of the roof.

The main façade

Detail in carved stone

Balcony

Window on the main façade

Guimard's signature on the façade

Windows on the main façade

Elevation of the side façade

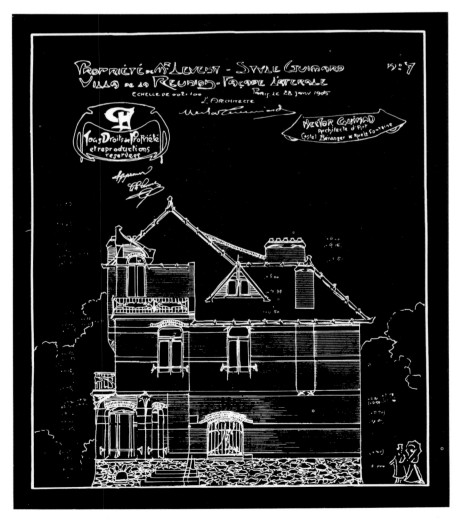

SUBURBAN VILLA

16 RUE JEAN-DOYEN
EAUBONNE (VAL-D'OISE)

1905

This villa built in 1905 reveals a certain weariness, as if the time had arrived for Guimard to leave behind the tropical and troubling shores of Art Nouveau. Not a trace of those treelike natural motifs so common with him in his earlier work, unless we count such details as the ravishing ironwork banisters in the form of lianas on the three steps leading to the kitchen door.

Here the brick so favored by Guimard, as by so many Symbolist architects, is largely dispensed with; it is used as an accent, underlining, for example, the courses of the chimneys. The rest of the house is entirely in siliceous sandstone, but the way the stones are pointed, with a bead of cement, is so distinct as to seem a caprice of the architect: did he insist that the mason leave those joints well in evidence to underscore the "informal" aspect of each block of stone? The result is a façade that could have served the painter Dubuffet as model for one of his abstract compositions.

Rear façade giving on the garden

Street number

Main façade

Kitchen door giving on the garden

Did Guimard build this merely to keep the wolf from his own door? No doubt, if we date the house between 1905 and 1907 on the basis of certain pieces of ironwork identical to those in the Jassedé apartment building, but eventually rejected by their inventor. This was a time when he produced a series of small houses, all very much alike, at Morsang-sur-Orge. Other than in the veranda behind the kitchen and the stuccoed decoration of the ceilings, the architect's touch is seen chiefly in the stairways and balconies with their cast-iron decoration so typically "Style Guimard."

Living room

Veranda

CHALET BLANC

1908

With the Chalet Blanc, Guimard moved a little further still from the Art Nouveau movement. The house is charming, airy, and, with its shallow-pitched roof and samurai window, would be just as much in its place looking out over the Pacific as on the shores of the Atlantic along the coast of Le Touquet.

At first sight the overall structure brings to mind certain of the Métro stations Guimard designed.

Nothing medieval here; the house is cheerful, carefree. The owner must have given his architect a free hand. His name was Blanc—white—and the house Guimard built for him is something of a play on words. The material is the usual siliceous sandstone and brick, but here the stone is razed flat and cut in large shapes, thus differentiating the house from so many others using the same materials that one sees on the outskirts of Paris.

With this villa Guimard drew singularly close to what his English, German, and Austrian colleagues had been doing. Lacquered wood plays a principal role, lending the whole a feeling of lightness and, at the same time, bringing out even more the Anglo-Saxon note so much to the liking of the French of the time.

The main balcony with its basket shape rather recalls the one on the Castel Orgeval, and the others are supported by wooden consoles cut as thin as shavings and so light as to seem easily swept away by the wind.

The sign over the front gate

View from the street

General view of the rear façade

Steps and main door

Below: A small ceramic dog—by the architect himself—stands guard. There were originally two dogs but one disappeared under mysterious circumstances a few years ago.

The front gate

In this last effort of an in-between period of uncertainties and experiments Guimard returned to his favorite materials: siliceous sandstone, brick, and wood. The forms are simple. At the most, here and there a volume seems to wish to escape from a strict alignment. Elsewhere, a few curves, but frigid and taut, still allow themselves a slight change in direction that carries over from wood to standstone. But one cannot help sensing that the architect did not believe in this house nor in the possibilities for developing volumes that the terrain itself offered. Certainly the house does not bear out the promise of something cheerful, even playful, suggested by the front gate with its design as absurd as an engraving by Escher—an invention both pleasing and convincing.

For a long time I wondered about the plaque in lava that identifies the house to the passerby. I have already said that for some years by then Guimard had given up working with outside collaborators, among them Eugène Gillet, his supplier of products in lava. Was this plaque an exception? Or, more simply, something reused?

The truth of the latter hypothesis is suggested by the history of the Villa La Surprise in Cabourg, which Guimard built around 1903. That villa was in fact built in two stages. Nothing surprising about that, since Guimard often did further work on buildings already completed, especially when they were his friends' homes. The transformations in Cabourg were extensive, involving the addition of an entire bay with a window high up to which the villa owed its name: it was the only spot from which one had the "surprise" of a view of the sea. But what was the house called before that major change? Two old postcards have the answer: Chalet Blanc! The plaque was simply removed and set aside for a time until the architect had the occasion to use it for another chalet painted white.

Clockwise, from upper left: Veranda; Small window on the rear façade; Balcony; Grill-work on ground-floor window

Balcony

HOTEL GUIMARD

122 AVENUE MOZART
PARIS 16E

1909-12

I know avenue Mozart like the back of my hand: twenty-five years of my life were spent on that thoroughfare. The development of avenue Mozart would well repay study, because it would show how little the streets of Paris have changed in the past hundred years. The avenue was opened in 1867 and soon became the main route for the inhabitants of Auteuil on their way to the center of the city. Aside from a few Second Empire buildings that have survived, private mansions have given way to taller buildings, most of them quite without character, although there are those handsome constructions which, if they are preserved, will be considered masterpieces three-quarters of a century from now.

It was avenue Mozart that Guimard chose as the site for a house of his own, one that could accommodate both living quarters and his studios. The result was one of his finest realizations. Compact, stocky, yet, so to speak, light on its feet, it gives the impression of being the elegant headquarters of a victorious army.

At first view one is struck by the architect's care in designing and positioning his windows and balconies. Defying rhyme and reason, they are each of a different cut, each placed where one would least expect it: witness the window on the third story, a quarter of which is situated on the precise corner of the building and which appears to be haughtily indifferent to the classically arranged bay on the story below. Of particular note in this regard is the long fourth-story balcony surmounted by two lanterns of a type frequently used by Guimard.

The entrance is superb: high, spacious, it could have been inspired by René Lalique's building at 40 cours la Reine (1905). The architect also took great pains with the façade that now faces on his Villa Flore (1924–2). Thus the large window on the top story that gave light to his wife's studio and the window on the ground floor that looks almost as if it supports the rest of the building with its four stone consoles are positioned symmetrically. The basic structure is in hewn stone, and though brick is still employed massively, its discreet colors make it less conspicuous.

More than elsewhere in Guimard's architecture, here one is none too sure what is rational, what irrational, and Guimard lives on in every inch of the building he erected as a home worthy of his wife, Adele Oppenheim, a talented American painter he married the year he began this hôtel.

In 1912, when the building was completed, Guimard was approaching fifty and still making every effort to top the market. But real estate developers were setting profit above beauty, and many of his designs lay fallow in his atelier. Running breathlessly to keep up with the new styles, he might catch up with them but never outstrip them. By 1937 he decided to leave France. He feared the war drawing ever closer; his wife was Jewish. He would try to make his way in New York, but with little success. He would die there in 1942 at the age of seventy-five. Who at the time still knew his name?

General View

At the start of 1909 Guimard married Adeline Oppenheim. This event, which might have been of no more than biographical interest, proved to be on the contrary of capital importance for the remainder of the groom's career: Madame Guimard was American, a painter in her own right, and brought with her a personal fortune that came like a gift from heaven to her husband, whose business had been going badly. The first consequence of the happy union revealed itself promptly: by June Guimard submitted his request for permission to build this new private residence for himself and his wife.

Guimard's changes of address closely paralleled changes in his stylistic development. Installing himself on the ground floor of the Castel Béranger was a deliberate move right at the start of his career as an avant-garde architect. To build a hôtel on the exclusive avenue Mozart and settle there no doubt marked his own awareness of a change in the direction of his career: his clients would no longer be the sort to be received in a modest-rental building decorated in an eccentric fashion which some found aggressive or worse but, thenceforth, in a hôtel particulier whose elegance spoke more of an eighteenth-century refinement than of medieval fantasy. In moving closer to rue de Ranelagh, where his friend Léon Nozal, with whom he had decided to engage in ambitious real estate operations, lived, Guimard once and for all would give up building his strange castles in the environs of Paris. Artistic satisfaction was one thing, but such villas brought him little in the way of either glory or cash.

The Hôtel Guimard was a new visiting card. Here the architect spoke a new and refined decorative language, ostensibly sober or at least well-balanced, and one with the obvious intention to charm, to seduce. Leaving behind a period of trials and mostly errors, making a place for himself in an appropriate social milieu where success in real estate speculation was what was appreciated, Guimard could no longer try to astound and shock with his outlandish ornaments and designs. Desirous of a firm place in the architects' world, he would do what he could to reconcile his obsessive pursuit of originality with the much more restrained and conservative taste of his potential clientele.

Opposite: Front door with the monogram of the architect and master of the house

Right: Façade giving on Villa Flore

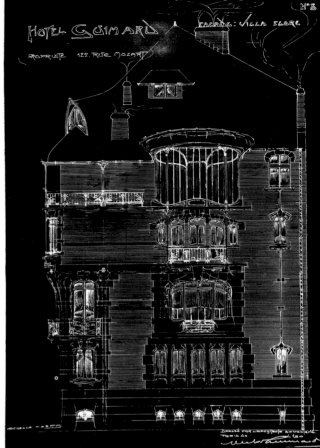

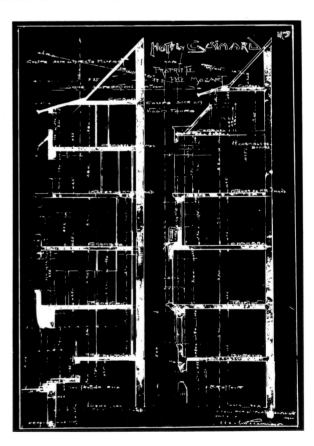

Section

Details of the balconies and windows

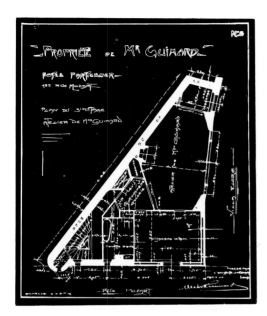

Plan of the top floor

Architectural plans and drawings

The way each floor of this hôtel is arranged remains perhaps the finest example of functionalism in all of Guimard's work. To gain space he simply dispensed with a main staircase on the grounds that it made a fine impression but took up valuable space, and he replaced it with an elevator, the ultimate symbol of modernity. Each floor had a separate function: architectural studios on the ground floor, reception rooms on the second, living quarters on the third, and on the fourth, lighted by an immense bay now totally redone, Madame Guimard's studio. Guimard's originality is most in evidence on the second floor, where a salon and a dining room, both oval-shaped, fit perfectly into the triangular shape imposed by the lot.

Opposite, above: Side elevation

Dining room (Period photograph; furniture now in the Musée du Petit-Palais, Paris)

Front elevation

Various exterior details

TREMOIS APARTMENTS

11 RUE FRANÇOIS-MILLET
PARIS 16E

1910

It would soon be thirteen or fourteen years since Art Nouveau threw academic architecture into confusion. Ten years after the Exposition Universelle of 1900, Guimard in these Trémois Apartments seems left behind by his times. The touch is still elegant, if more stripped down than before. Bow windows are abandoned in favor of a discreet projection of the windows, and the glazed surface area on the main façade is increased so as to get more light in living quarters that give on a quite narrow street.

With the French still disdaining brick as a "cheap" material, Guimard had to resign himself to giving it less importance. The building itself is less massive overall and escapes the monumental look of the apartments Guimard built in those same years on rue Agar, some hundred yards distant.

A narrow frontage created particular problems. Moreover, the adjoining buildings as we see them now are not exactly architectural delights: on one side, a public establishment, a day nursery built around 1880 and showing it all too plainly; on the other, a decidedly ordinary building in the style of 1922–23. The main façade of the Trémois Apartments is composed of three vertical units: the one on the left is distinguished by a broad window on each floor; the middle section has slightly curving balconies that already hint at the style of the synagogue Guimard would build a few years later; on the right the general look is rather more like what is customary in the neighborhood.

Thanks to its ironwork the building nonetheless has a charm of its own. The architect lavished his utmost inventive imagination on the balconies, whose grilles are treated like openwork embroidery.

A drawing of this façade served as publicity for Guimard's "products," turned out by the Saint-Dizier foundry. The Trémois apartments furnished a perfect demonstration of the importance of metal for ornamental elements, which probably explains the great number and the diversity of windows on the front of the building. In point of fact, what originality the Trémois building has resides in the many different combinations of the different models of prefabricated ironwork utilized, chosen from among the most elegant and refined in the catalogue, in contrast with the Hôtel Guimard, which preceded it and whose charm lies as much in the elaborate stonework as in the arrangement of the volumes or the decoration of the windows.

General view

Detail of ironwork

A window on the first floor

A door handle

The front door, in glass and wrought iron

HOUSING COMPLEX

**17, 19, 21 RUE LA FONTAINE;
8, 10 RUE AGAR; 43 RUE GROS**

PARIS 16E

1909-11

The impressive group of apartment buildings Guimard erected on rue La Fontaine and two smaller cross streets was completed in 1911. The first result was a new street opened on the occasion, initially called—appropriately—rue Moderne, and later given the name of the actress Léonie de Charvin, known as Agar, who had lived for years in Auteuil.

Here again there were a great number of difficulties to cope with. To begin with, there was the competition only a few yards distant of his own Castel Béranger and, a little farther, of the ravishing Hôtel Mezzara. This is, in fact, very much a Guimard neighborhood, and once again he had to face the problem that obsesses every great creator, to prove that what he had done fifteen years before, which had made him one of the apostles of modernism, could still be surpassed, and that his creative spirit had not been worn away by the intervening years.

The façades on rue La Fontaine and the side street are in hewn stone, and brick is absent even from the doorways. Perhaps the time for arabesques was past. Certainly there is infinitely more rigor here than in Castel Béranger. Yet there are still medievalist reminiscences, with plantlike colonnettes that spring from the tops of doors to encircle the windows above with floral decoration. On the part giving onto rue Gros a group of rounded bow windows discreetly swell out the façades. Once again brick is obsessively present, earth-colored, baked in a slow kiln: as always Guimard concerned himself with every detail.

Ironwork was still in fashion, and here it has resisted wear and weather. The balconies all around the buildings are still as beautiful, as surprising, as they must have appeared at the time they were installed. There are other wonderful details: the typically Art Nouveau storefronts and the plaques giving the street name, rue Agar, which are masterpieces of lettering.

Corner building, rue La Fontaine
and rue Agar, in hewn stone

Window, 19 rue La Fontaine

General view of the building at the corner of rue Gros and rue Agar

Café at 17 rue La Fontaine, which has preserved its original front

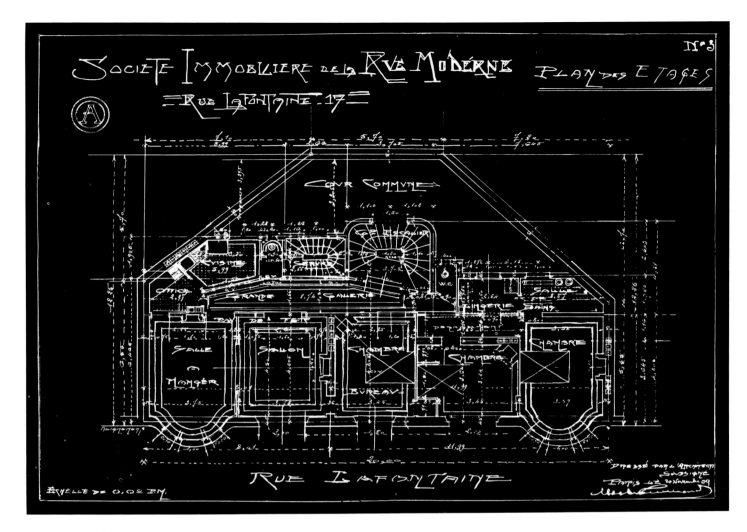

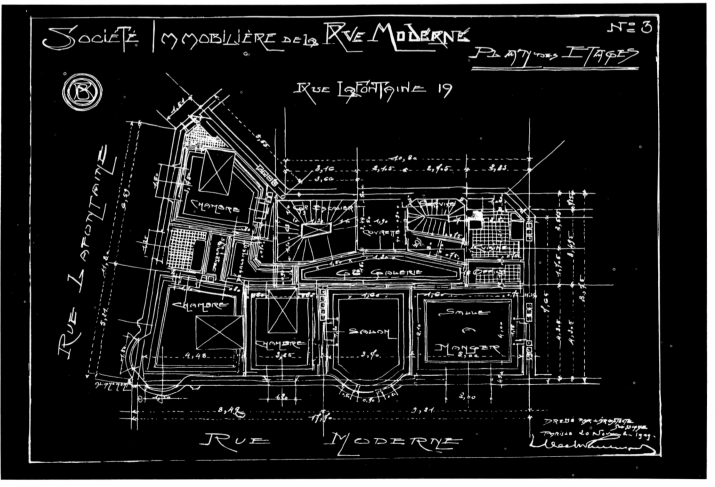

Ground plans of 17 and 19
rue La Fontaine

General view of the buildings at 43 rue Gros (at the left)
and at 17 and 19 rue La Fontaine

Balcony on the second floor, recalling a tree with its roots

Façades on the rue Agar in brick and hewn stone

After private homes and apartment buildings the architect proposed his idea of a "cité Guimard" which involved opening a new street and parceling out its lots. The idea was to exploit land owned by Léon Nozal, to prove that Guimard's new orientation was not only viable but also aesthetically satisfying and harmonious and that a wealth of detail in no way distracted from the overall unity. The "readability" of the present buildings—long dismissed as decadent but in fact carefully calculated—is based on two simple principles: verticality and the use of artistic cast-iron ornamentation. Along with these the architect played infinite variations on each of his components (doors, windows, roofs), to the point that we are led to take all the buildings to be very similar though they are in fact each very different. Thus, for example, only the unit on rue Gros has markedly projecting bow windows and a crowning element that looks for all the world like some barbarian helmet.

The demonstration would no doubt have been even more convincing if the project had been carried through as planned. Of the eleven buildings initially envisaged only six were erected. Those on rue Agar were intended to be accompanied by two others; the triangle on rues Agar, Gros, and La Fontaine was to have been built entirely by Guimard but the fourth building was realized very much later by another architect; and there were to have been two buildings opposite 43 rue Gros. No more than sixty percent of this building program was finally realized. Had it gone through as conceived it would have been Guimard's major work and his only fully consistent large-scale project. As it happened, all of his future projects of this type remained on the drawing board or ended up as isolated constructions.

Detail of the façade of 17 rue La Fontaine

Details of buildings in the complex

HOTEL MEZZARA

1910

Here we have one of the most successful of Guimard's town houses, as handsome as the central ornament of an admirable mantelpiece. The structure is already in the architect's late style; the exterior at least still belongs to the world of Art Nouveau.

The house takes its distance from the street, set off from it by an ironwork fence as fine as a woman's hair-net. The façade is slightly off-angle by something like ten degrees. With its three tiers of windows, it calls to mind an athlete who catches his breath before lifting his weights that fraction of an inch higher. The front door is positioned asymmetrically on the right. On the left, the architect took advantage of a small space to make room for the concierge's loge. With its sloping overhang the doorway is decidedly medieval in look.

Brick wins out massively over hewn stone here. The day of sandstone has ended. The ironwork is superb and recalls the decorations on the façade of the Trémois Apartments.

The interior arrangement is a masterwork of grace and harmony. An extraordinary stained-glass skylight, especially designed to illuminate the main hall where Monsieur Mezzara, a textile manufacturer, displayed his models, softens and diffuses the light of day. And the staircase? Its like has never been seen. With its asymmetrical base it makes one think of the cautious step-by-step progress of some mythical animal faced by the new problem of climbing stairs.

General view

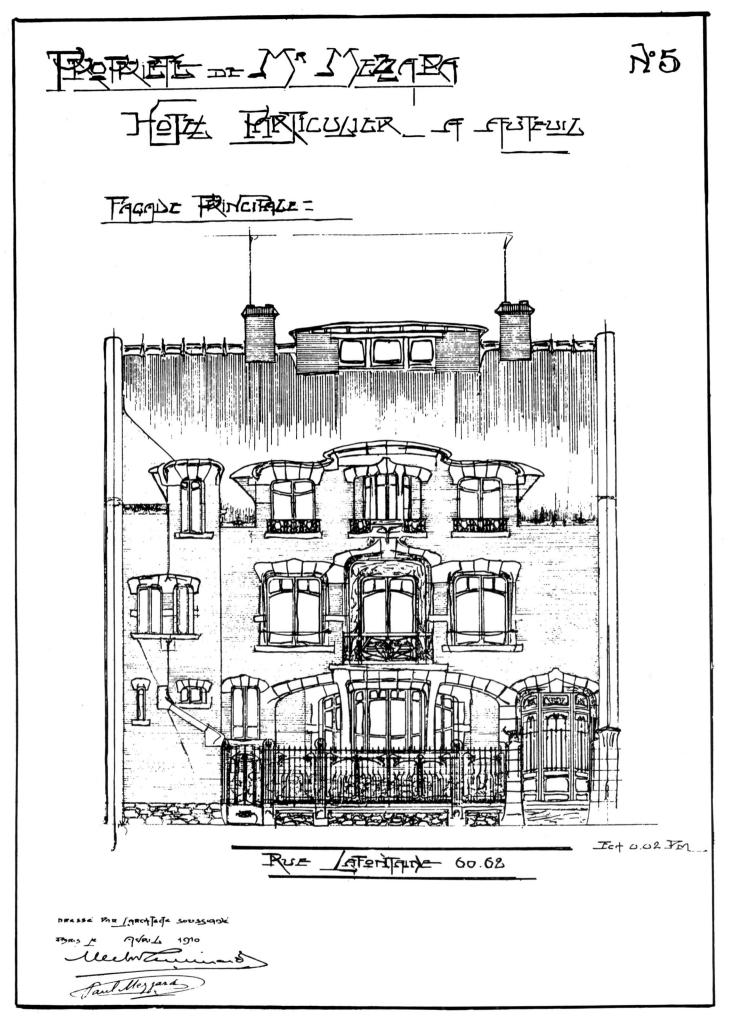

Elevation of the main façade

Elevation of the rear façade

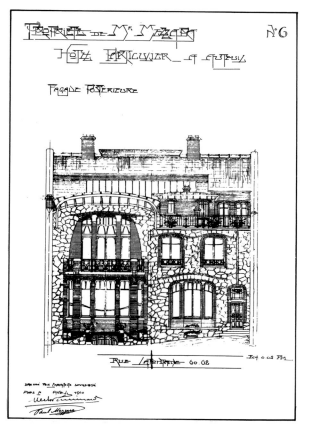

Rear façade on the garden

Grand hall

Stained-glass skylight

Wooden balustrade of the staircase in the vestibule giving onto the grand hall

Paul Mezzara, industrialist and creator of embroideries and laces, exhibited at the salon of the Société des Artistes Décorateurs along with his friend Guimard. The town house that Guimard designed for him can justly be considered the last small gem of our architect's career. We can be thankful that the house has been exceptionally well preserved. It is, in fact, the only one of Guimard's creations to retain the full ensemble of floor tiles, lighting fixtures, stained-glass windows, fireplaces, furniture, and metal fittings. And this although the property has changed hands several times and has been used for quite different purposes.

As Guimard had done a number of times since his Hôtel Jassedé, the building is set back from the street and thus allows for a small front court closed off by a grille in which standardized cast-iron elements were used together with others in wrought iron and in plant forms especially created for the hôtel. The somewhat overly sober symmetry of the façade is broken up by a small wing that projects at the left.

The principal and unifying space of the house as a whole is the front hall, a vast area in constant use as passage and as organizing point for all the household activities. It is the necessary connection between the rooms giving onto the street, those facing the garden, and the service rooms and corridors that occupy the lateral wing. Particular pains were taken with the decoration. This includes a large stained-glass skylight providing natural light directly from above, an especially elegant staircase with elements in cast or wrought iron, which makes its impression without being overly conspicuous, and the doors whose ornamented glass insets were forerunners, in their geometrical simplicity, of a new aesthetic that would reach its climax only after the war. Most remarkable, to my mind, is the idea of juxtaposing highly refined forms molded in stucco with bare metallic elements where every rivet is left plain to see. Nowhere did Guimard more effectively reveal the structural framework of a building, nor did he ever succeed better in drawing from it an aesthetic solution: look at the slender metal stems that, in threes, come off a main stem and spread across the ceiling to form a girdle around the very beautiful skylight.

Detail of the mirror over the mantel

Cast-iron fireplace in a small parlor overlooking the street

Door at the base of the staircase

An inside door

SYNAGOGUE

10 RUE PAVÉE
PARIS 4E

1913

In Paris in the twelfth and early thirteenth centuries the Jews possessed two synagogues. It took six hundred years of persecution before Napoleon authorized them in 1808 to open more. By 1900 Paris had scarcely more than ten synagogues, and they were edifices without character. The temple on rue de la Victoire, for example, erected at the end of the Second Empire by the architect Aldrophe, is every bit as insipid as those many mission churches built everywhere in France in the same epoch.

Rue Pavée has twelve centuries of history behind it. Narrow, gloomy, not much used now, it was once inhabited by people of fashion: chamberlains of Charles VI, counselors to kings. There were hôtels that belonged to Henri II of Lorraine, at number 12 lived the Comte de Brienne, at number 24 the Conseiller Lamoignon and, very much later, the poet Jacques Delille. Today the neighborhood is frequented mostly by Jews of North African and Central European origin, modest people who have remained firm in their faith.

It was a bold but happy initiative of the old Parisian congregation to call on Guimard to raise their new temple.

The task was difficult, as the street is narrow. The façade was conceived as a kind of stylization of the Holy Book itself. Not the slightest ornament except for a kind of rippling, like an open page of the Bible ruffled by the breath of devotion. The only decorative elements are the Star of David and a stylized frieze framing the main door and, directly under the roof, the Tablets of the Law. Between the windows are panels ornamented with an abstract design recalling the Gothic linenfold motif.

In its proportions the temple is theatrical, haughty, sorrowful perhaps. The interior may be the most medieval of all those realized by Guimard and, in its way, recalls the Humbert-de-Romans Auditorium. Here we are not far from Viollet-le-Duc's reconstructions: old dreams dreamed by men nostalgic for the grandeur of time past.

Façade

A door handle

The central door

The fact that his wife was Jewish may explain the presence of a synagogue among the works of Guimard, who, at the start of his career, had built so much for the Catholic circles of Auteuil. Here his private and professional lives came together with fine results.

The lot available for the synagogue had its difficulties, located as it was precisely where the very narrow rue Pavée makes a bend. Once again the solution lay in setting the façade a good six and one-half feet back from the street.

The austere exterior scarcely prepares one for the elegant interior with its calculated volumes, cast-iron ornaments, painted and gilded stuccoes. Certain of the metallic elements were selected from among the models in the Saint-Dizier catalogue conceived for funeral monuments, and it does seem as if the architect-designer was making one last try to prove that these Style-Guimard castings could serve anyone for any purpose and in any place: by that date it was becoming all too obvious that those prefabricated elements had not really caught on and that their inventor himself remained one of the very few to utilize them.

View of the interior

Window

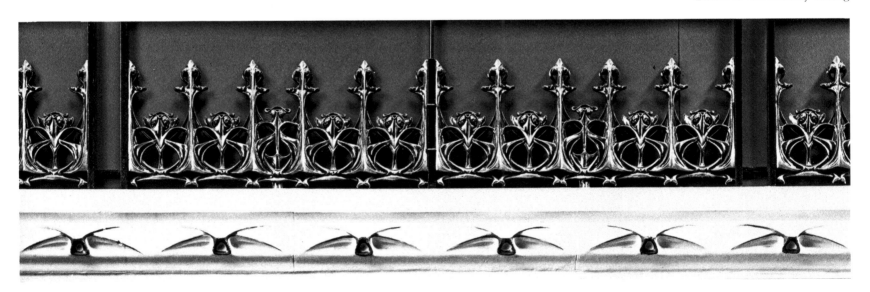

Elevation

Opposite: Detail of the galleries

Detail of the balcony railing

VILLA HEMSY

⬭ **3 RUE DE CRILLON**
SAINT-CLOUD (HAUTS-DE-SEINE) ⬭

1913

Guimard built the Villa Hemsy on the slopes of Saint-Cloud, in a neighborhood of elegant and spacious dwellings, most of them in Anglo-Norman style, that was every inch the equal of such stylish resorts as Cabourg, Deauville, and Trouville.

The façade is composed of three sections. The entrance at the left shelters under horizontal wooden beams and recalls that of the Chalet Blanc. The central section projects like the tall prows of those sailing ships which, in the seventeenth century, assured the Dutch the mastery of the seas: in place of portholes, seven windows, three on the ground floor, two on the second floor, two under the eaves where the front juts forward like a poop deck. The two-storied right wing is surmounted by a peaked roof set back and enclosing a double window. The side of the house, in the simplicity of its brick inlays and its asymmetrical windows, once again reveals the architect's taste for the medieval.

The villa is faced with siliceous sandstone and soft brick in light colors. There is no longer a trace of ceramics, and the ironworker has certainly lost his inspiration: Guimard's characteristic flowery arabesques are replaced by a simple solar motif.

Art Nouveau is over and done with. On the outside, at least. Inside, from the moment you cross the threshold you find it still in full bloom. The door is surprisingly handsome with its six motifs incised in the wood and drawn in the manner of the ornamental capitals in old manuscripts. The staircase too remains in the tradition of the Gothic cabinetmaker, with the banister and the foot of the stairs simulating a piece of cloth. It is in the special treatment accorded the doors and windows that the visitor finds here, however briefly, the architect's own genial touch.

It is, alas, all too certain that this house has been the victim of later, often destructive modifications. Although no document shows us exactly how it was originally, it is obvious that the right bay in particular was entirely rebuilt and its windows redone. Fortunately, the most original elements do survive: the strange peaked roof a whole story high and the overhanging balcony held up by two wooden crutches. It is not impossible that, for this villa in Saint-Cloud, Guimard thought back to what he had done in his Modern Castel in Garches. The enveloping roofs are given similar importance, as are the supporting structures in wood. The single essential difference resides in the fourteen years that separate the two houses: the time for castles and follies has passed; now Guimard wishes henceforth to please more than to shock.

General view

OFFICE BUILDING

10 RUE DE BRETAGNE
PARIS 3E

1914

The appearance of Art Nouveau was closely bound up with economic upheaval and changes in the style of living. That evolution is reflected in the look of our city streets, where we find an exact image of fashions and fancies, however ephemeral they may have been, and a thousand bits of evidence of the way the ordinary people lived to whom the city owes its existence.

The first big department stores were opened well before the end of the century. Zola, in his novel *Au Bonheur des Dames*, traces the history of one of those gigantic establishments which, like a powerfully tentacled monster, reaches out and swallows up the little shops around it.

To counter that threat shopkeepers had to make an effort to render their premises attractive, to give them an air of distinction, a personality very different from the facelessness and uniformity of the big stores. For that, they had to have recourse to everything modern decoration could offer: show windows, publicity signs, lighting effects. The creators of such boutiques had at their disposition an entire repertory of new forms they could exploit with utmost freedom. In small shops wooden frames were used for the showcases that had to be repeatedly opened and shut. Metals, notably cutout copper, and other new materials brought colorful accents. Façades took on a lively and showy look, and their diversity broke the monotony of the streets.

This office building is very different from anything on Guimard's familiar rue La Fontaine. The rue de Bretagne is very old and still has houses from the seventeenth and eighteenth centuries. To a neighborhood traditionally devoted to commerce and crafts Guimard would attempt to bring a touch of modernity. The building opens on the street through a doorway topped by a bare pediment devoid of grace. The façade comprises four main sections, two flat, the other two with only slightly projecting bow windows. What fantasy there is is almost confined to the topmost story, with the corner giving onto rue Condé topped by a sort of overhanging roof. Two columns or, more accurately, pilasters, serve as both support for the roof and decorative motif. Otherwise, 10 rue de Bretagne has not the slightest flourish of decoration, neither on the main door nor on the façade. The building is constructed on a base of freestone one scarcely notices, and the rest is in a pale gray brick which makes for a certain monotony.

The edifice is not signed, and one wonders if it even deserved to be.

Certain details still show Guimard's unmistakable hallmark, and a few ideas, notably at roof level, are particularly attractive. But the general impression explains why the building has never been anyone's particular favorite. The overly angular volumes have no place in Guimard's language. Awkwardly—and, moreover, a little late in the day—the architect was trying to catch up with Auguste Perret and Henri Sauvage. The juxtaposition of diverse materials no longer involves any break in surface, any surprise: all too sober, they lack charm. Can all this be ascribed to the fact that the building was begun only after the start of the war and doubtless built in haste? Or to the way the shops at street level have been modernized? More simply, more truthfully perhaps, we must blame a temporary inability of the architect to think in new terms, to take hold again. By then it was obvious that the apartment building project on rue Agar would never be completed and that a similar project on rues Robert-Turquan and Henri-Heine was already running into difficulties. Once again Guimard's prospects were bleak. The synagogue, the Villa Hemsy, and this office building are evidence of one more period of doubt and gestation such as he had gone through in the past. Common to those periods are particularly austere and sober façades: hesitations between a past over and done with and a still-unfathomable future.

HOTEL

3 SQUARE JASMIN
PARIS 16E

1922

The building is dated 1922. Though Guimard was by then well past fifty, he continued to show a taste for Art Nouveau as well as a persistent nostalgia for a medieval world forever moribund, forever reviving. He was of the race of those who regret not having been born at the close of the fifteenth century: in their hands the Gothic would never have expired.

The medievalism is underscored here by a few motifs framing the broad windows on the left as well as by the linenfold motif on the stretch of wall beneath the second-floor bow window. For all his long-standing passion for the court of Charles VI and the feudal burgs as imagined by Victor Hugo, however, Guimard was resolved to remain a modernist. World War I had just ended. Paris had had its ordeals. In four years great numbers of houses had fallen into half-ruin. They had to be torn down, rebuilt quickly and inexpensively. Guimard had ambitious projects, but unfortunately the wind was blowing in other directions. And yet, a house like this is sure proof of a still-vigorous talent. He himself designed these horizontally laid binding stones and had them cast in concrete. The horizontal grooves on their surface look for all the world like music staffs on which every passerby can write, mentally, his own song.

This astonishing dwelling is one of Guimard's last true creations. Despite the recession he would still, however, be given other commissions, among them even large-scale apartment houses.

General view

Bow window on the first floor

The end of the war brought Guimard new enthusiasm. New buildings and rebuildings were in demand everywhere. And there was only one way to do them: fast and on the cheap. Guimard promptly set to work figuring how to satisfy those two imperatives without sacrificing quality, beauty, the use of decoration. He demonstrated his findings in this house on Square Jasmin, as he would do later and on a grander scale at the Paris Exposition of 1925 when, in a few days, he erected a model town hall in the French village (though without the consequences he had anticipated). This little pavilion and the apartment building on rue Henri-Heine are all that remain of Guimard's activity in the area bounded by the rues Jasmin, Henri-Heine, du Docteur-Blanche, and de l'Yvette; a garage on rue Robert-Turquan and a small private hôtel on rue Pierre-Ducreux have only recently been torn down.

The fanlight over the front door

Detail of the basement window

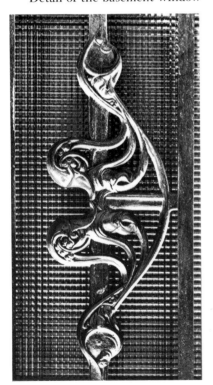

Wrought-iron balustrade on the first-floor bow window

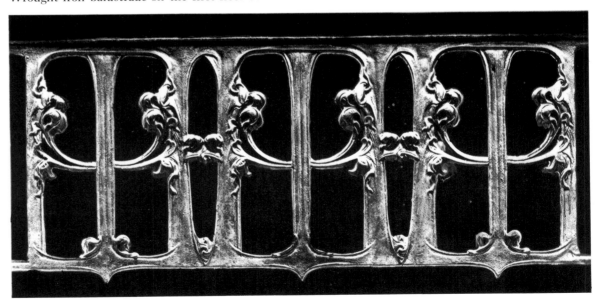

VILLA FLORE

120 AVENUE MOZART
PARIS 16E

1924-26

In its decoration and structure this apartment building succeeds in integrating itself into the overall architectural look of the neighborhood. It holds its place modestly, as if the presence of the spectacular Hôtel Guimard across the street intimidated it. With a particularly narrow main front—it is a mere eleven and one-half feet wide—it does little to catch one's attention.

The façade on the avenue Mozart is notable for its two bow windows, on the third and fourth stories, and for the single room on the corner of the building one story from the top. When this room is illuminated, it brings to mind the top of a lighthouse or an observation post at the summit of a citadel. The façade on the tiny street called Villa Flore is designed in a more classical manner. The rear façade with its access to the service rooms is rather unoriginal, and even the motifs of the balustrades are repeated identically.

On the avenue Mozart side of the building, freestone predominates, though here and there bricks are inserted at the base of windows like firing holes in a fortress. The lateral frontage on rue Villa Flore is dominated by slightly pinkish bricks in varying shades interrupted here and there by motifs in ceramic or stone.

There is no longer anything of Art Nouveau here. The general style announces the coming of Art Déco.

All in all, a disappointment, and this is confirmed by a small detail characteristic of all of Guimard's late constructions: the building next door, at 122, his own Hôtel Guimard, is proudly signed and dated; 120 bears no such identification. He was content to mark his role as master builder by no more than a pretty plaque in cast iron with the words "Villa Flore" in white on blue enamel.

Top: Plaque on the street

Above: Third-floor bow window

On a narrow lot opposite his own hôtel Guimard experimented with what would remain
his style for the rest of his career: firmly emphasized vertical structures, angular projections,
and abrupt breaks in rhythm. But, above all, a
virile monumentality without precedent in his
work.

General view

APARTMENT HOUSE

18 RUE HENRI-HEINE
PARIS 16E

1925-28

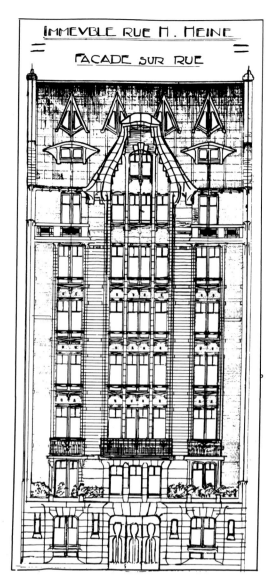

Elevation of the main façade

Here we have a turning point in Guimard's production. Art Nouveau was dead and forgotten. Instead, architects were looking to the Bauhaus, and this apartment building can be thought of as the aging architect's salute to the new times. Yet the trained eye will recognize another homage, and one with many years of history: that of a follower of Viollet-le-Duc to his long-deceased master. Indeed, what we have here is, in plain fact, one more provocative attempt to bring about one more medievalizing revival.

On the central corps a single window recalls Guimard's customary bow windows, while the ironwork grillage is of the same character as that on the Trémois Apartments and the Hôtel Guimard. The building is in stone and brick, of a construction beyond reproach yet quite lacking in warmth. The end of an era of enthusiasms? Did Guimard sense that his day was over and that his place would be occupied thenceforth by Americans?

The project for the development of a vast terrain bounded by the parallel rue de l'Yvette and rue Henri-Heine originated around 1910, the date of two buildings put up by Henri Preslier, one of the architects involved in the operation. Up to 1926 Guimard had succeeded in building there no more than three modest constructions, among them the little house on square Jasmin. There was not much to show for sixteen years of property development: it had proved very difficult to attract a clientele to the neighborhood.

Guimard may have had two reasons for raising this building on his own. Answerable to no one else, for once he need not worry about a client's wishes and requirements. By building in that so far unsuccessful area he no doubt hoped, put

Partial view of the façade

Stained-glass window
on the staircase

Pottery plant holder
at the front door

crassly, to start the ball rolling. On the other hand, it is decidedly significant that he should take entire responsibility for a project at exactly the moment when his new style was taking shape. In doing so, he renewed the personal commitment he had already made in building a hôtel for himself at 122 avenue Mozart in the immediate neighborhood. Unfortunately, what he hoped for did not come about and he would never again build in the vicinity.

Here again certain details strike one as reminiscent of earlier constructions (call it "fidelity to a style" if you wish): the prefabricated castings, stonecarvings, and glass bricks he used as far back as the Castel Béranger; a staircase banister which seems a simplified reminiscence of the one in the Hôtel Mezzara. Yet all those elements are perfectly integrated into a work of a new and different time. From his past, Guimard would preserve those avant-garde elements no one had yet surpassed.

Corridor with conspicuous Art Déco elements

The staircase

APARTMENT HOUSES

1926-29

The Exposition des Arts Décoratifs—where the new style of Art Déco was given its baptism and blessing—has been and gone: from now on, architecture will look toward the United States. Here in fact the photographer has caught Guimard's buildings at 36 and 38 rue Greuze in a manner that recalls huge New York buildings rather more than anything in Paris. The only concession to fantasy is the irregular disposition of the windows across the façade and the presence of a few bow windows. But the builder's talent is still in evidence in a detail that tells much about the financial difficulties of the time: the gutters and rainpipes in Eternit cement nobly disguised as antique columns, a modern adaptation that would not have displeased Viollet-le-Duc.

1926: the Great Depression was just around the corner. The watchword was "economy." Except for the underpinnings in stone and the supports of the balconies this entire building is in brick. What is more, all the bricks are of the same color and are duller in tone than those Guimard favored in earlier years.

Who would ever think that these apartment houses were built by the man who, twenty-five years earlier, had conceived the Castel Béranger? One senses that he took no satisfaction from this undertaking: you will look for his signature in vain.

General view

Twinned windows

The last works by Guimard to come down to us—his country house at Vaucresson has been demolished—are the buildings on rue Greuze, and they are a kind of final homage to his favorite material, brick. To it he added the Eternit tubing perfected by his friend and colleague Henri Sauvage to make an impressive vertical partitioning. Little is known about the background of this project except that once again a group of individuals contributed capital and terrain to a company especially set up to carry it through. Since the war Guimard had put up only four buildings, two of them in prefabricated materials. All his real estate development projects had foundered, nothing came of the inventions he patented, and his career came to an end with two works of fine quality, not lacking in originality and grace but which one must admit would never catch our attention if Guimard were not their author. Yet, merely passing by, one never suspects how very limited the lot was he had to work within, not even twelve feet deep, and how, to gain space, he ingeniously extended certain accessory rooms, bathrooms in particular, by the use of bow windows. At seventy Guimard showed no slackening in his inventive curiosity.

Details of the façades of 36 and 38 rue Greuze

Small window on the first floor of number 36

General view

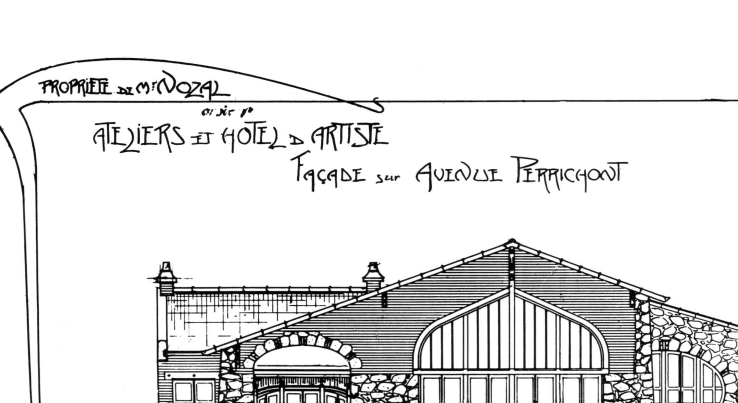

PROPRIÉTÉ DE M. NOZAL

ATELIERS ET HOTEL D'ARTISTE
Façade sur Avenue Perrichont

N° 4

Echelle de 0.02 . 1.00

PARIS 22
L'ARCHITECTE

STUDIO
Avenue Perrichont, Paris 16e
1903

*Among Guimard's destroyed works the studio
on avenue Perrichont deserves particular notice. For one, it shows how very diverse were
the buildings that Léon Nozal commissioned—fate has willed it that none survive—
and, for another, it is evidence of a particularly
fruitful and happy but all too brief period in
Guimard's life. The architectural drawings all
indicate that this hôtel was intended for an artist: the fact is, for Guimard himself. It was
designed to provide accommodations for part of
his agency, his professional quarters in Castel
Béranger having grown too small for all the
collaborators his projects now required.*

CASTEL HENRIETTE
Sèvres (Hauts-de-Seine)
1899

In itself, what was this Castel Henriette? One of the numerous small "follies" of Guimard's all-out baroque period, no doubt neither more successful nor more beautiful than the others. Nonetheless, as we can still see it in old photographs, its tower—very soon pulled down by the architect himself—gave it a special cachet as something at once playful and conspicuously original. When the house was first threatened with destruction and then in fact torn down in 1969, it became above all a symbol. It was hailed as a masterpiece, though it quite certainly was that to a lesser degree than the Salle Humbert-de-Romans or the Castel Orgeval. Now, when all the pleas and shouting are over, it can be said that, without in any way admitting its necessity, the destruction of the Castel Henriette at least proved useful in making a broader public than that of the connoisseurs aware of Guimard's architecture, in leading them to love it and, thus, help preserve it.

DECORATIVE IRONWORK

Various types of grilles and balustrades in cast iron, produced by the foundry at Saint-Dizier

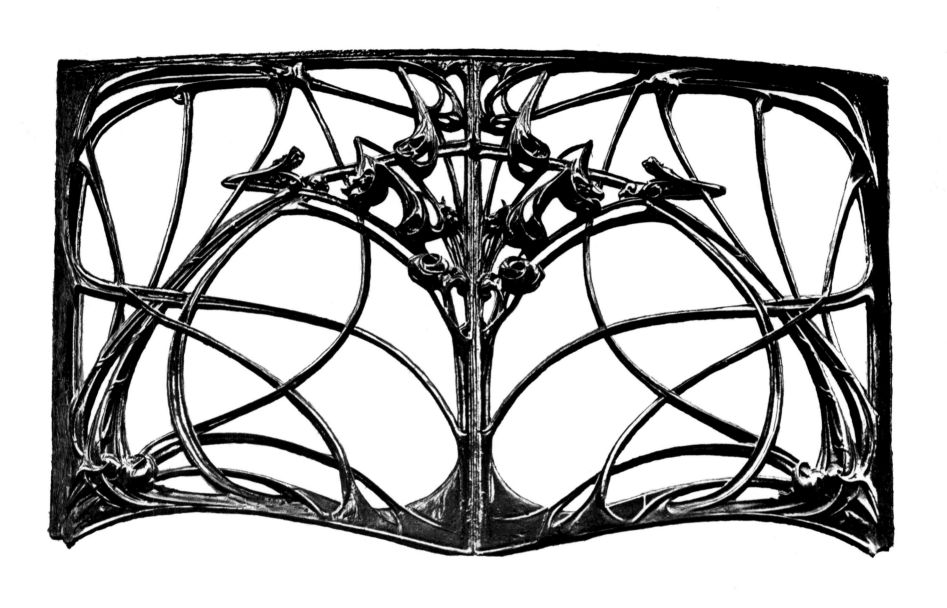

CEMETERY MONUMENTS

Guimard, like the American Louis Sullivan and the Italians Raimondo D'Aronco and Giuseppi Sommaruga, designed a few cemetery monuments. For him it was an elegant way to render homage to a few among those who, in their lifetimes, had given him their confidence. Here then we see the monuments of such great clients as the Jassedé family and Charles Deron-Levent, who was also his old friend.

The taste in funerary monuments revealed here, these new ways of treating an old form, were the fruit of an alliance between Symbolism and atheism or paganism. Free of all dogmatic constraint, new believers in the spirit held that they more than others were truly responsive to human woe. As a result, at the start of this century a new type of small monument began to appear in the burial grounds of great cities, some giving eloquent expression to the various tendencies of Art Nouveau.

Detail of the cross on the Caillat family tomb, Père-Lachaise Cemetery

Nothing is harder to invent than a funerary monument! Almost without noticing it one can slip from the trivial into the grotesque, to say nothing of all the possible gradations in the way of ugliness, tearful bathos, and plain bad taste.

Those designed by Guimard could pass as simple exercises in style if the names we find on their upright slabs were not, often, those we know as his patrons. Such monuments date from the finest moments of his career and afford further evidence of his changes in style and aesthetic. Thus that of the Obry-Jassedé family goes back to his first phase, and while the vertical element is much like what one finds in his first buildings, the jardiniere already suggests the weird animal forms that swarm across the Castel Béranger. The Caillat monument with its flowing and complex lines is typical of the unmistakable "Style Guimard." For the Deron-Levent family he devised something with the same exquisitely simple elegance as the hôtel he built for them. And, finally, the monument for Albert Adès has the geometric simplicity of the architect's last works.

Tomb of the Caillat family, 1899, Père-Lachaise Cemetery

Tomb of the Obry-Jasse-dé family, 1895, Issy-les-Moulineaux Cemetery

Tomb of Albert Adès, 1922,
Montparnasse Cemetery

Tomb of Charles Deron-Levent, 1912,
Auteuil Cemetery

DECORATIVE ARTS

Guimard as interior decorator, cabinetmaker, furniture maker, *ensemblier*, to use the term of the time. Because of the essential scenic conception he had of his work, he never ceased to concern himself with the slightest details: doorknobs, keyholes, door and window handles, banisters; in all of them he was a man of the avant-garde. Prophetically, he already had the idea of the human environment as a totality to which the proponents and practitioners of "design" aspire today. Except that, to my knowledge, no one since Guimard has succeeded in creating furniture of greater beauty: one need only think, among so many examples, of the bureau of the Hôtel Guimard, now in the Musée de l'Ecole de Nancy, or the chair his widow donated to the Cooper Union Museum (now the Cooper-Hewitt Museum), New York.

For Guimard a building had to be a whole whose parts, however insignificant to an outsider's eye, must fit perfectly into the overall aesthetic conception. To conceive a façade without at the same time imagining what would go behind it was unthinkable for Guimard. Whatever he built bore his hallmark on everything down to the least details. Not that it was easy or always possible to impose that standard on, say, an apartment house, but he could have his way with a villa or a private hôtel. This explains why after creating the most diverse models for Castel Béranger—everything from furniture to metal fittings—he concentrated above all on the decoration of private homes, at least up to World War I. For the apartments of his large rental projects he limited himself to supplying stucco cornices, fireplaces, doors, and occasional stained-glass windows. Thus his most celebrated and handsomest pieces of furniture, those that account for his reputation today as one of the greatest masters of furniture design of his time, come from his own home or that of Léon Nozal, though he designed pieces for both the Castel Val and the Hôtel Mezzara.

Armchair in pearwood from the dining room of the Hôtel Guimard

Chair in pearwood from the dining room of
the Hôtel Guimard

Buffet in pearwood from the dining room of Hôtel Guimard

THE HÔTEL GUIMARD FURNITURE

The furniture of the Hôtel Guimard was donated by the architect's widow to three museums: the bedroom to the Musée des Arts Décoratifs in Lyon; the study to the Musée de l'Ecole de Nancy, which specializes in Art Nouveau; and the dining room to the Petit-Palais, Paris. In all these pieces Guimard showed his delight in using fruitwoods, in supple forms, and in ornaments in embossed leather, as on the chairs where an O and a G, his wife's and his initials, are interlaced. Never were Guimard's beloved shell motifs, knotworks, and slender filletings confided to a more sensual material: pearwood responded perfectly to all his linear inventions, and thanks to its color, grain, and luminosity, it gave them a fluid, almost living dynamism. This very likely explains why he soon gave up the darker and less lustrous woods, mahogany in particular, that he had used in the Castel Béranger.

Dining room of the Hôtel Guimard

Fireplace-buffet in the Coilliot house, Lille. The fireplace is
in enameled lava, the buffet in pearwood with enameled glass

Ensemble comprising a fireplace in enameled lava with mirror and two small pearwood sidepieces

THE MAISON COILLIOT FURNITURE

The two fireplaces in the Maison Coilliot are unquestionably the strangest and most hauntingly beautiful creations of all of Guimard's career as decorator. It was with a real zest that he mingled enameled lava, glass, and wood in structures that are no less functional than decorative and are built permanently into the house itself, which is one reason they have survived in place. Their almost plantlike shapes strike everyone who sees them, and the stunning nervous lines of their various winding and twining verticals are eloquent evidence of what sets Guimard apart from "Style Nouille"—Noodle Style—the wicked but nonetheless justified derogatory name applied to Art Nouveau when it descended to the facile and mawkish.

THE HÔTEL MEZZARA FURNITURE

The dining room of the Hôtel Mezzara is the last complete ensemble still in place with all its buffets and table and chairs as well as an elegiac wall painting by Charlotte Chauchet-Guilleré, who, like Guimard and Mezzara, was a regular participant in the Salon des Artistes Décorateurs. Still using his beloved pearwood, here Guimard signed his last known and identified set of furniture.

Stoneware vases from forms created by Guimard in 1899, height 27.5 cm. (10⅞ in.)

VASES

After his success with Castel Béranger, Guimard—for the moment the darling of Paris—was sought after by various manufacturers to create models especially for them. Of these, the state manufactory at Sèvres was the most prestigious, and for it he created three models: a monumental jardiniere, a flower-pot holder, and a vase in which he fully exploited the procedure of crystallization to achieve an extraordinarily rich finish. These pieces were presented at the Salon des Artistes Décorateurs in 1904 along with a large showcase for bibelots and objets d'art which Guimard designed in order to have his productions better displayed in the manufactory shops and which unfortunately cannot be found today.

THE MILLOT PERFUME BOTTLE

Another isolated creation, commissioned in the same circumstances as the models for Sèvres, was the perfume bottle designed for the Millot company. The motifs, the calligraphy on the label, and the very abstract stopper make a strange composition much like—on a vastly smaller scale—what one finds on the façade of the Coilliot house. Nothing here, and certainly not the very curious shape of the bottle itself, could have come from a mind other than Guimard's: it is a tiny but eloquent product of an all-embracing imagination without its match in the past.

CHRONOLOGY

In this chronology, the current street address is given for existing buildings by Guimard. For unbuilt projects and destroyed buildings, old street names are used, although these may have been changed in the intervening years. We have indicated in each case if the building was never built (NB), altered (A), or destroyed (D), with the date in the latter two cases if known. All other buildings are still in existence as of this writing. All buildings are in Paris unless otherwise noted.

Where possible, each work is dated as of the request for permission to build, which symbolizes the end of the conception and the beginning of the realization of a project. Otherwise, the date of the blueprints or, by default, any available information (the date on the façade or cornerstone, bibliographical data) has been used to date projects.

Works not dated with precision are placed at the end of each year. Guimard's postcards, chronicling the "Style Guimard" up to 1903, are placed in relation to the building illustrated on each card (p. 1, etc.). Works illustrated and discussed at greater length in the book are cross-referenced (q.v.).

This chronology would not have been possible without the friendly assistance of Mr. Ralph Culpepper, whose personal archive was invaluable.

G.V.

1867   March 10: Hector Germain Guimard born in Lyons, son of Marie-Françoise Bailly and René Guimard.

1882   Guimard enters the Ecole des Arts Décoratifs in Paris (studio of Charles Genuys).

1885   Receives diploma at the Ecole des Arts Décoratifs, and enters the Ecole des Beaux-Arts (studio of Gustave Raulin). He participates in its competitions until 1893.

1887   Places tenth in a design competition for the Hôtel de Ville de Calais. Volunteers in the army (33rd artillery regiment).

1888   First building: Café-Restaurant "Au Grand Neptune," 148 quai d'Auteuil (now quai Louis-Blériot), for Mrs. Grivellé (D, 1909).

1889   Pavillon de l'Eléctricité, Exposition Universelle (D).

1890   Living at 147 avenue de Versailles. Participates in his first Salon.

1891   June: Villa Toucy, Billancourt, for Mr. Lécolle (D). July: Hôtel Roszé, 34 rue Boileau, with Aimé Octobre, sculptor, and Emile Müller, ceramist (q.v.). October: Two pavilions at 145 avenue de Versailles for Mr. Hannequin (D, 1926).

1892   January: Placed in charge of a course in drawing at the Ecole des Arts Décoratifs. Also in 1892: Tomb of Victor Rose, Batignolles Cemetery, with Alfred Lenoir and T. Guérin, sculptors.

1893   June: Hôtel Jassedé, 41 rue Chardon-Lagache (formerly rue du Point-du-jour) and 9 grande avenue de la Villa de la Réunion, for Louis Jassedé, with Emile Müller, ceramist (q.v.; p. 12). September: Maison Jassedé, 63 avenue du Général de Gaulle, Issy-les-Moulineaux (formerly 63 avenue de Clamart, Vanves), for Charles Jassedé.

1894   Guimard leaves the Société des Artistes Français and joins the Société Nationale des Beaux-Arts. Living at 64 boulevard Exelmans. Summer: First trip to England. August: Mirand-Devos Chapel and Devos-Logié Chapel, Gonards Cemetery, Versailles, with T. Guérin, sculptor. September: Hôtel Delfau and furnishings, 1-ter rue Molitor, with T. Guérin, sculptor, and Emile Müller, ceramist (q.v.; A, 1907). October: Small building constructed from the ruins of the old Church of Auteuil at the presbytery, 4 rue Corot, for the Société Historique d'Auteuil et de Passy (A).

1895   February: First request for a building permit for the Castel Béranger (called the Castel Fournier), for Mr. Fournier. Spring: Enlargement of the studio of the sculptor Carpeaux, 39 boulevard Exelmans (q.v.). March: Ecole du Sacré-Coeur, 9 avenue de La Frillière (formerly 15), for the Société des Immeubles destinés à l'Education et la Récréation de la Jeunesse (q.v.). Only the main building survives, while the porter's house, lavatories, and fences have been destroyed. June: Second request for a building permit for the Castel Béranger, on behalf of Mrs. Fournier. Summer: Guimard travels to England, Scotland, Holland, and Belgium, where he meets Paul Hankar and Victor Horta. Fall: Castel Béranger and furnishings, 14 rue La Fontaine (formerly 16) and the Hameau Béranger, with Ringel d'Illzach and Raphanel, sculptors; Eugène Gillet, lava; and Alexandre Bigot, ceramist (q.v.; p. 4 and 10). Also completed in 1895: Giron, Mirel, and Gaillard tombs, Montparnasse Cemetery; Chapel for Rouchdy Bey Pacha (née Sophie Leveillon), Gonards Cemetery, Versailles; Tomb for the Obry-Jassedé family, Issy-les-Moulineaux Cemetery.

1896   Before April: Projects for the Exposition Universelle of 1900, including an artificial hillside with theaters, restaurants, and a windmill (NB). August: Interior designs for the salon of "The Melrose," 16 rue Saint-Lazare and for the Théâtre de la Bodinière, 18 rue Saint-Lazare, for Mr. Bodin (it is not known if these were executed). September: Villa La Hublotière, 72 route de Montesson, Le Vésinet, for Mr. Perrin (q.v.).

1897   At the beginning of the year, Guimard moves into the Castel Béranger. May: Boutique Couttolau, boulevard de Saumur (now boulevard du Maréchal-Foch), Angers (D), and a porch in ceramics for a house for the Exposition de la Céramique et des Arts du Feu, with Raphanel, sculptor, and Bigot, Gilardoni, and Brault, ceramicists (D; p. 7). Also completed in 1897: Tomb of Nelly Chaumier (location unknown) and interior decorations for Mr. Roy of Gevrils, some of which are in the Musée d'Orsay, Paris.

1898   June: Hôtel Roy, 81 boulevard Suchet (D, 1954; p. 20). September: Salle Humbert-de-Romans and|the Lacordaire youth club, 58–60 rue Saint-Didier, for the Société des Immeubles de la Rue Saint-Didier, (D, 1905, except for the organ, which was moved to Saint-Vincent-de-Paul in Clichy; p. 5 and 22). October: Pavillons Rocher, 9 and 9-bis impasse Racine, Hameau Boileau (A, c. 1965). Also in 1898, Guimard completes work on the Castel Béranger and publishes L'Art dans l'habitation moderne: Le Castel Béranger, 1894–98, and begins work on the Maison Coilliot (completed 1900), 14 rue de Fleurus, Lille, for Louis Coilliot, with a lava façade by Gillet (q.v.; p. 15).

1899   April 4–May 20: Castel Béranger exhibition at the offices of Figaro. April: Modern Castel (now known as Villa Canivet), 18 rue Alphonse-de-Neuville, Garches (A, c. 1937–38; p. 3). May 12: Guimard lectures on "The Artistic Renaissance in Modern Architecture," at the offices of Figaro. Also in 1899: Tomb for the Ernest Caillat family, Père-Lachaise Cemetery, Paris (q.v.); Villa la Bluette and furnishings (known as La Houle since 1938), rue Pré-de-l'Ile, Hermanville-sur-Mer, Calvados, for Prosper Grivellé, with lavawork by Gillet (q.v.; p. 9 and 23); Castel Henriette and furnishings, 46 rue des Binelles, Sèvres, for Mrs. Hefty (q.v.; D, 1969, architectural elements in the Musée d'Orsay, Paris; p. 6 and 13); the beginning of Guimard's association with the Manufacture de Sèvres, for whom he created three vases and a large showcase (now lost); and the cover of the first issue of the Revue d'Art.

1900   January: Plans for a popular university for the 15th arrondissement (NB). April: Opening of the Exposition Universelle, Paris, with various minor works by Guimard, including showcases for E. Déjardin, a booth for M. Charles, and the Revillon-Millot perfume bottle. July: Guimard resigns from the Ecole des Arts Décoratifs, and is placed in charge of the street entrances of the Métropolitain. In total, 141 street entrances were installed up until 1913. The main stations (Etoile and Bastille) were destroyed, but two smaller stations (Abbesses and Porte Dauphine) remain (q.v.; p. 2 and 11). November: A small watchman's pavilion and stores, 10–12 impasse Boileau (now rue Parent-de-Rosan) for E. Déjardin (D). Also about 1900, a house at Versailles (location unknown).

1901   November: Opening of the Salle Humbert-de-Romans.

1902   April: Housing, offices, and warehouse for the Etablissements Nozal, 132 avenue de Paris (now avenue du President-Wilson), Saint-Denis (D, 1965; p. 21).

1903   Beginning of the year: Castel Val and furnishings, 4 rue des Meulières, quartier de Chaponval, Auvers-sur-Oise, for Mr. Chanu, with Bigot, ceramist (q.v.). March: Jassedé Apartments, 142 avenue de Versailles and 1 rue Lancret, for Louis Jassedé (completed 1904, q.v.). April: Artist's studio and hotel, recorded as 12 (but later renumbered 6) avenue Perrichont extension, for Léon Nozal (D, 1961). This studio was constructed for Guimard's own use, and he occupied it until 1918. July: A summer pavilion in a park in the "Style Guimard," Exposition de l'Habitation, Grand-Palais, Paris (D; c. p. 1). It is on this occasion that the phrase "Style Guimard" is first used, and Guimard publishes (in November) 24 postcards. October: Opening of the first Salon d'Automne, of which Guimard is a founding member. October 27: Guimard lectures on "Art in Contemporary Housing." December: Project for a Monument du Souvenir Français (NB). Also around 1903: Enlargement of the Castel Henriette, Sèvres; Villa La Sapinière (summer apartments), 10 rue Pré-de-l'Ile, Hermanville-sur-Mer, Calvados, for Mr. Barthélemy (q.v.; A); Chalet Blanc, 22 avenue Aristide-Briand, Cabourg, for Léon Nozal (D); and a memorial for Paul Nozal, near Barbezieux (D?).

1904   January: Opening of the first Salon des Artistes Décorateurs, of which Guimard is an active member. February: Watchman's booth for the Hôtel Nozal (completed 1906), 52 rue du Ranelagh (D, 1957). March: Hôtel Nozal and furnishings, 52 rue du Ranelagh (completed 1906), for Léon Nozal (q.v.; D, 1957; some furnishings in the Musée des Arts Décoratifs, Paris). May: Projects for country houses. September: Castel d'Orgeval, 2 avenue de la Mare-Tambour, Villemoisson, for M. Laurent (q.v.). October: Project for raising the height of a hôtel, 2 rue Chardon-Lagache, for Mrs. Gireaux (NB?).

1905   February: Hôtel Deron-Levent, 8 grande avenue de la Villa de la Réunion (completed in 1907, q.v.).

1906   July: Project for raising the height of an apartment house, 25 rue Erlanger, for Mr. Ledru (NB). Also about 1906: Cottage Clair de Lune, 18 rue du Muguet, parc Beauséjour, Morsang-sur-Orge (A) and Villa Rose d'Avril, avenue de la Pépinière, parc Beauséjour, Morsang-sur-Orge (D?).

1907   July: Annex for the Hôtel Roy, 81 boulevard Suchet (D, 1954). End of the year (?): Enlargement of the Chalet Blanc, Cabourg, which is henceforth known as La Surprise; Chalet Blanc, 2 rue du Lycée and 1 rue Lakanal, Sceaux (q.v.). Also in 1907: Publication by the Saint-Dizier Foundry of a catalogue of castings in the Style Guimard. About 1907: Suburban villa, 16 rue Jean-Doyen, Eaubonne (q.v.); Furniture and garden door with glass roof, 5 bis avenue Foch, Saint-Cloud, for M. Desagnat (the roof was destroyed with the building; the door is in the Musée d'Orsay, Paris).

1908   June: Project for raising the height of the offices of the Etablissements Nozal, 9 quai de Passy (D).

1909   February 17: Guimard marries Adeline Oppenheim, known as Addie. June: Hôtel Guimard and furnishings, 122 avenue Mozart and 1 villa Flore (q.v.). The interior has been altered, but after World War II, Mrs. Guimard donated the dining-room furnishings to the Musée du Petit-Palais, Paris, the master bedroom furnishings to the Musée des Arts Décoratifs, Lyons, and the study furnishings to the Musée de l'Ecole de Nancy, in Nancy. August: Trémois Apartments, 11 rue François-Millet (q.v.).

1910   April: Hôtel Mezzara and furnishings, 60 rue La Fontaine, for Paul Mezzara (q.v.). May: The first series of buildings for the housing complex in the rue Moderne, now the rue Agar, for the Société Immobilière de la rue Moderne, including Building D at 43 rue Gros and 2 rue Moderne (Agar), Building B at 19 rue La Fontaine and 6 rue Moderne (now 9 rue Agar), and Building A at 17 rue La Fontaine. Also belonging in this first series, although unbuilt, are plans for Buildings C, E, and F at 1, 3, and 4 rue Moderne. July: Apartment house, 148 quai d'Auteuil (now quai Louis-Blériot) at rue Téniers, for Prosper Grivellé (NB). September: Apartment house, 147 quai d'Auteuil (now quai Louis-Blériot) at rue Téniers, for Prosper Grivellé (NB).

1911   Spring: As vice-president of the Société des Artistes Décorateurs, Guimard participates in the debate concerning the project for an Exposition Internationale des Arts Décoratifs, which will be finally decided in 1916, but will not take place until 1925. Also in 1911, a new series of apartment houses are constructed in the rue Agar, by the Société Générale des Constructions Modernes: Building I at 9 (then 7) rue Moderne (now 10 rue Agar), Building H at 7 (then 9) rue Moderne (now 8 rue Agar). Buildings K and L, planned for 12 rue Agar, are not built.

1912   Guimard moves into his hôtel in the avenue Mozart. Tomb of Charles Deron-Levent, Auteuil Cemetery (q.v.). About 1912–13: Villa Hemsy, 3 rue de Crillon, Saint-Cloud (q.v.).

1913   Synagogue, 10 rue Pavée, for the Association Culturelle Israélite Agoudas Hakihilos (q.v.). Project for the rue du Docteur-Blanche.

1914   February: Hôtel, 7 rue Pierre-Ducreux (now rue René-Bazin) and rue Robert-Turquan, for Mrs. Nicolle de Montjoye (D, c. 1960). Also in 1914: Office building, 10 rue de Bretagne (completed in 1919, q.v.) and a project for town houses in the rues Henri-Heine, Jasmin, Pierre-Ducreux, and Robert-Turquan for the Société Immobilière des Constructions Modernes (partly built in 1921, see below).

1915   March: Guimard prepares a paper on the question of rents during the war.

1918   December: Guimard requests permission to use sheds near the Orangerie in the Parc de Saint-Cloud. In 1968, approximately 2,000 plans and drawings are found there.

1920   February: Automobile garage, rue Robert-Turquan, for the Société Générale des Constructions Modernes (D, c. 1966). July: Project for adding to the Hôtel Barthelemy, 53 rue du Ranelagh (D). Also in 1920–21: Projects for workers' houses made with prefabricated materials for provinces devastated by the war.

1921   April: Small hôtel, 3 square Jasmin (formerly passage Jasmin), for the Société Générale des Constructions Modernes (q.v.). Built with prefabricated materials in a few days.

1922   Tomb of Albert Adès, Montparnasse Cemetery (q.v.). Guimard is a cofounder of the Groupe des Architectes Modernes.

1923   November: Project for tourist hotels, boulevard Gouvion-Saint-Cyr, by the Groupe des Architectes Modernes, including Guimard, Sauvage, Richard, Sézille (NB).

1924   March: Villa Flore, 120 avenue Mozart and 2 villa Flore, for Michel Houyvet (q.v.).

1925   April: Opening of the Exposition Internationale des Arts Décoratifs, with a town hall for a French village and a small chapel for a cemetery by Guimard (D).

1926   March: Apartment house, 18 rue Henri-Heine (completed 1928; q.v.).

1927   January: Apartment house, 36 rue Greuze, for the Société Civile de la rue Greuze (q.v.).

1928   January: Apartment house, 38 rue Greuze, for the Société Civile de la rue Greuze (q.v.).

1929   Guimard receives the Legion d'Honneur.

1930   Summer: Guimard proposes a competition for a monument to commemorate the victory of the Marne, near Sezanne (NB). Also about 1930: Country house, called "La Guimardière," rue Le Notre, Vaucresson (D, March 1969), and projects for museums constructed from prefabricated materials (NC).

1938   September: The Guimards arrive in New York.

1942   May 20: Hector Guimard dies in New York.

ACKNOWLEDGMENTS

My very cordial thanks go to those persons who collaborated directly or indirectly in the realization of this book which, without them, would have been impossible to complete:

Mr. Maurice Rheims, of the Académie Française, who consented to write the preface and texts; Mr. Georges Vigne who was willing to write descriptive captions and the chronology at the back of the book. I am equally indebted to Mr. Vigne for the loan of precious documents, some of them previously unpublished.

The owners of buildings and private homes built by Guimard, who kindly permitted me to photograph their premises, both outdoors and indoors, including Mr. and Mrs. Hervelin; Mr. and Mrs. Rocher; Mrs. Aranovitch; Mrs. Perrin; Mr. and Mrs. Mathiot; Mrs. Pinoteau; Mr. Coilliot; Mr. Dehemme; Mr. Le Cornu; Mr. and Mrs. Le Cornu; Mr. and Mrs. Moreau; Mrs. Mennesson; the synagogue of the rue Pavée; Mrs. Haydée Martin-Candellier and Mrs. Aliette Vandevoorde; the headmistress of the Foyer de Lycéennes, 60 rue La Fontaine.

The Musée du Petit-Palais in Paris and its director Mrs. Burollet; Miss Sophie de Bussière; the Archives of the city of Paris; the Bibliothèque Forney and its director Mrs. Anne-Claude Lelieur; the Parfums Revillon/Millot company and Miss de Marjorie; Mrs. Ragon of Lille; Mr. Igielnik of the Paris Métro administration; Mr. Landon and Mr. Alain Dols; the Musée National de Céramique in Sèvres; Mr. Alexis Chatin; the Central-Color laboratory which supplied and developed my Ektachromes; and many more.

To all, with all my heart: Thank you.

To make good an injustice I must also mention Mr. Ralph Culpepper even if he did not collaborate directly on the book.

Thanks to him a large part of Guimard's work has been preserved from ineluctable destruction, notably documents, plans, drawings, furniture, and bibelots. He literally snatched from the hands of ignorant persons and vandals furniture doomed to end as firewood.

That American with a passion for Guimard and Art Nouveau covered all of France during thirty years, tracking down a gable-end, a fragment of ceramic, a faded scrap of wallpaper, a crumpled sketch, anything and everything bearing the master's imprint. He even identified certain houses built by Guimard whose owners had no idea of their architect's name. With utter unselfishness Mr. Culpepper has deposited in the Musée des Arts Décoratifs, Paris, a great number of documents to which, unfortunately, I was not granted access.

The photographs were taken with a Linhof Master-Technika 4-x-5-inch camera.
Lenses: Super-Angulon 75 mm and 90 mm, Symmar 150 mm, and Téle-Xenar
      360 mm made by Schneider-Kreuznach.
Films: Ektachrome and Ilford FP4.

PHOTOGRAPH CREDITS

DATE DUE

APR 1 9 2000			
MAR 1 8 2002			
MAR 2 8 2003			
NOV 1 6 2003			
GAYLORD			PRINTED IN U.S.A.